Basic and Advance Python Programming Language

NIPA GENX ELECTRONIC RESOURCES & SOLUTIONS P. LTD.
New Delhi-110 034

About the Authors

Dr Agya Ram Verma was born Ayodhya, Uttar Pradesh, India. He received the B. Tech degree in Electronic and Instrumentation Engineering from IET MJPRU Bareilly, UP, India, in 2010. He completed the M.Tech. degree in Electronic and Communication Engineering from the Indian Institute of Information Technology (IIIT), Design and Manufacturing, Jabalpur, India. He received the PhD degree from Uttarakhand Technical University, Dehradun, in 2019. He joined the Department of Electronics & Communication Engineering, G. B. Pant Engineering College, Pauri Garhwal, India, in 2013, as Assistant Professor. His research interest includes machine learning, signal processing. He has published more than 35 research papers in refereed international journals and conferences. He has published one Patent in 2021. He has published one book on fundamental of machine learning form Sara book publication in 2021. He also obtains one R&D Project and one Constancy Project. He is also reviewer of many reputed international journals like Computer Methods in Biomechanics and Biomedical Engineering: Imaging & Visualization (Taylor & Francis), IET Generation, Transmission & Distribution, International Journal of Signal and Imaging Systems Engineering (IJSISE), Journal of Intelligent & Fuzzy Systems, GUCON 2019 IEEE Conference, India, Signal processing journal, Electronics Letters, IET.

Dr.Yatendra Kumar is former Head and Associate Professor, Department of Electronics and Instrumentation Engineering, Faculty of Engineering and Technology, Mahatma Jyotiba Phule Rohilkhand University, Bareilly, UP (India). He has completed his B.Tech (Electronics and Instrumentation Engineering) in 1999 and M.Tech (Instrumentation Engineering) from National Institute of Technology (Formerly known as Regional Engineering College), Kurukshetra, Haryana in 2001. He has completed his Ph.D. degree from Indian School of Mines (ISM), Dhanbad. He has more than 20 years of teaching experience. Besides, he has authored and co-authored several research papers published in national and international journals. He is also reviewer of many reputed international journals like IEEE Access, International Journal of Electronics, Microwave and Optical Technologies Letter, International Journal of Electronics and Communications(AEU) International Journal of RF and Computer Aided Design (RFCAD) and International Journal of microwave and Technologies.

Dr. Sag Ram Verma received his B.Sc. in 2003 from Dr. R. M. L. Awadh University, Ayodhya, India and M.Sc. in 2005 with Mathematics from Banaras Hindu University, Varanasi, India. He received his Ph.D. in Applied Mathematics from Indian Institute of Technology (BHU), Varanasi, India in year 2009. He is currently working as an Assistant Professor in Mathematics, Gurukula Kangri (Deemed to be University), Haridwar (UK) India since 2011. His research interest includes Mathematical programming, Wavelet analysis and its applications. He has published more than 25 research papers in refereed international journals and conferences. He has guided 4 PhD student.

Basic and Advance Python Programming Language

Agya Ram Verma
Assistant Professor
Department of Electronics & Communication Engineering
G. B. Pant Institute of Engineering and Technology
Pauri-Garhwal, Uttarakhand, India

Yatendra Kumar
Former Head and Associate Professor
Department of Electronics and Instrumentation Engineering
Faculty of Engineering and Technology
Mahatma Jyotiba Phule Rohilkhand University
Bareilly, Uttar Pradesh, India

Sag Ram Verma
Assistant Professor
Gurukula Kangri (Deemed to be University)
Haridwar, Uttarakhand, India

NIPA GENX ELECTRONIC RESOURCES & SOLUTIONS P. LTD.
New Delhi-110 034

NIPA GENX ELECTRONIC
RESOURCES & SOLUTIONS P. LTD.
101,103, Vikas Surya Plaza, CU Block
L.S.C.Market, Pitam Pura, New Delhi-110 034
Ph : +91 11 27341616, 27341717, 27341718
E-mail:newindiapublishingagency@gmail.com
www: www.nipabooks.com
For customer assistance, please contact
Phone: + 91-11-27 34 17 17 Fax: + 91-11- 27 34 16 16
E-Mail: feedbacks@nipabooks.com

ISBN: 978-93-91383-63-3

Composed and Designed by NIPA.

Acknowledgements

Our debts in the writing of this book are many, and we spell them out now. Bear with us. We acknowledge many in the 'References' section towards the end of the book. We have tried our best but almost certainly failed to recognize some of the others by not making proper notes. To any such creators that we may have overlooked, our apologies. We have learned a great deal from the writings of experts in the investor/trader community and the Python community on online forums like stackoverflow.com, quora.com, and others and are indebted to them.

Finally, we would like to thank all the students we have taught in the past several years. A special thanks to those of you who endured our first few iterations of the lectures before we learned how best to teach it. Dear students, we exist because you exist. You have inspired us, challenged us, and pushed us never to stop learning just to keep up with you. We hope you enjoy reading this as much as we enjoyed writing it for you.

A.R. Verma
Y. Kumar
S.R. Verma

Preface

This book will introduce you to the python programming language. It's aimed at beginning programmers, but even if you have written programs before and just want to add python to your list of languages.

The first eight chapters explain python's basic and you should read them in order. The later chapters show how Python is used in specific application areas such as the web, database, networks, and so on, read them in any order you like. Chapter 1 this chapter explain different basic topic related python programming. Chapter 2 in this chapter define python operator. Chapter 3 in this chapter define looping statement. Chapter 4 in this chapter define python function. Chapter 5 in this chapter explain string statement. Chapter 6 in this chapter define list in python programming. Chapter 7 in this chapter explain tuple in python programming. Chapter 8 in this chapter explain dictionary in python programming. Chapter 9 in this chapter explain numpy in python programming. Chapter 10 in this chapter exaplain lambda function in python programming. Chapter 11 in this chapter explain pandas in python programming. Chapter 12 in this chapter explain python pandas functionality. Chapter 12 in this chapter explain data frame basic functionality. Chapter 13 in this chapter explain python pandas statical functions. Chapter 14 in this chapter explain python panda visualization. Chapter 15 in this chapter exaplain data visualization in python programming. Chapter 16 in this chapter explain object oriented programming. Chapter 17 in this chapter explain module in python programming. Chapter 18 in this chapter explain python library. Chapter 19 in this chapter explain turtle grapics in python programming. Chapter 20 in this chapter explain brief tour of the standard libray.

A.R. Verma
Y. Kumar
S.R. Verma

Contents

1

Basic Concept of Python Programming

1.1 Introduction

Python is an interpreter, high level, general purpose programming language developed by Guido Van Rossum and its first version was released in 1991. There are two major Python versions: **Python 2 and Python 3**. Both are quite different.

1.2 Beginning with Python Programming

1.2.1 Finding an Interpreter

Before we start Python programming, we need to have an interpreter to interpret and run our programs.

Windows: There are many interpreters available freely to run Python scripts like IDLE (Integrated Development Environment) that comes bundled with the Python software downloaded from http://python.org/.

Linux: Python comes preinstalled with popular Linux distros such as Ubuntu and Fedora. To check which version of Python you're running, type "python" in the terminal emulator. The interpreter should start and print the version number.

macOS: Generally, Python 2.7 comes bundled with macOS. You'll have to manually install Python 3 from http://python.org/.

1.3 Compiler Vs. Interpreter: Explore What is the Difference Between Compiler and Interpreter?

Both interpreters and compilers are programs that convert the Source Code (high-level language) into machine codes (so that the computers can understand them). In this chapter, we will discuss the difference between Compiler and Interpreter.

A typical computer program usually exists in high-level languages that a human can understand. Thus, they contain various phrases and words from the English language (or any other in common use). Computers, on the other hand, cannot understand these languages as we do- but can comprehend a program in binary codes. As a result, we first write a program in a high-level language (source code), convert them into machine language, and make them readable for the computers. It is exactly when we need interpreters and compilers.

1.3.1 What is a Compiler?

A compiler is a translator that produces an output of low-level language (like an assembly or machine language) by taking an input of high-level language. It is basically a computer program used to transform codes written in a programming language into machine code (human-readable code to a binary 0 and 1 bits language for a computer processor to understand). The computer then processes the machine code for performing the corresponding tasks.

- Compilers check all types of errors, limits, and ranges. Thus, it's more intelligent.
- The run time of its program is longer, and it occupies more memory.

1.3.2 What Is an Interpreter?

It is a program that functions for the translation of a programming language into a comprehensible one. It is a computer program used for converting high-level program statements into machine codes. It includes pre-compiled code, source code, and scripts.

- An interpreter translates only one statement at a time of the program.
- They create an exe of the programming language before the program runs.

1.3.3 Difference Between Compiler and Interpreter

S.No.	Compiler	Interpreter
1	It scans the entire programs first and translate it into machine code	It sacns the program line by line and translate it into mechine code
2	Compiler show all errors and warning at same time.	Interpreter show one error at a time
3	Error occurs after scaning the whole program	Error occurs after scaning each line
4	Debugging is slow	Debugging is faster
5	Execution time is less	Execution time is more
6	Compiler used by language such as C, C++ etec.	An Interpreter is used by language such as python, Java etec.

1.4 Why to Learn Python?

It's growth is quite high. It is widely being used many fields like:

- Data analysis
- Machine learning
- Deep learning
- Artificial intelligence
- Desktop application development
- Web development etc.

1.5 What is Python IDLE?

After installing python just go to start menu and find will find "IDLE (python 3.7)". IDLE stands for integrated development learing environment. This is a by default development environment for python. There are many more development environments like pycharm, Eclipse, Eric etc.

1.6 Writing Program in Python

Python provides us the facility to write python program in one file that will be executed line by line sequentially. Steps for writing python program:

1. Open python IDLE.
2. Click on "File Menu" and then choose "New File".
3. A new screen/window will appear.
4. Here type the python program and save the program with ".py" estension.
5. To run the program click on "Run" menu and click on "Run Module"
6. The python code will start running

Example

Print()
This function is used to print message/ values.
Syntax:
Print("Hello")
Output: Hello
a=5
b=6
c=a+b

```
print(c)
output:11
```

Note: If any value print as it is the write inverted comma otherwise without inverted comma.

Till the previous examples, We have just printed the values stored in variables or directly printed the message. Now what if we want to print message along with values? Have a look on the code below:

Example

```
a=5
b=10
c=a+b
print("addition=",c)
```

If extending the previous program to know more about print method we may extend it as:

Example

```
a=5
b=10
c=a+b
print("addition of",a,"and",b,"=",c)
```

Input()

Python provides us the facility to take input from user using Input() function. This function prompts the user to input a value.

Example:

```
Name=input("Enter your Name")
Print(Name)
Example:2
Name=input("Enter your Name")
Print("Welcome Mr.",Name)
Output: Welcome Mr.Anup Kumar
```

Note:Please note that the Input() accepts the input only in string format. So, if any mathematcical calculation is to integer format. For converting the input to integer format python provide us a function called: int()

Example

```
a=int(input("Enter 1st value:"))
b=int(input("Enter 2nd value:"))
c=a+b
print("addition=",c)
```

1.7 Variable in Python

Variables are used to store values. But the best thing in python is that, unlike other programming languages, python has no command for declaring a variable. A variable is created as son as we assign a value to it.

For example:

```
X=5 # Here x is the type of int
Y="Ram Kumar" # Here x is the type of string
Print(x)
Print(y)
```

1.7.1 Variable Rules

A variable name cannot be anything as we want. There are some rules which has to be taken care while declaring a variable

- A variable name must start with a letter or the underscore character.
- A variable name cannot start with a number.
- A variable name can only contain alpha-numeric characters and underscores (A_z, 0_9, and_)
- variable names are case-sensitive (age, Age are different variables)
- There cannot be a space among variable name.

Example: Legal variable names

```
Myvar="hima"
My_var="him"
myVar="him"
MYVAR="him"
Myvar2="him"
```

Example:Illegal variable names

```
2myvar="him"
My-var="him"
My var ="him"
```

1.8 Python Language : Advantages and Applications

Python is a high-level, interpreted, and general-purpose dynamic programming language that focuses on code readability. It has fewer steps when compared to Java and C. It was founded in 1991 by developer Guido Van Rossum. Python ranks among the most popular and fastest-growing languages in the world. Python is a powerful, flexible, and easy-to-use language. In addition, the community is very active there. It is used in many organizations as it supports multiple programming paradigms. It also performs automatic memory management.

1.8.1 Advantages

1. Presence of third-party modules
2. Extensive support libraries(NumPy for numerical calculations, Pandas for data analytics etc)
3. Open source and community development
4. Versatile, Easy to read, learn and write
5. User-friendly data structures
6. High-level language
7. Dynamically typed language(No need to mention data type based on the value assigned, it takes data type)
8. Object-oriented language
9. Portable and Interactive
10. Ideal for prototypes – provide more functionality with less coding
11. Highly Efficient(Python's clean object-oriented design provides enhanced process control, and the language is equipped with excellent text processing and integration capabilities, as well as its own unit testing framework, which makes it more efficient.)
12. (IoT)Internet of Things Opportunities
13. Interpreted Language
14. Portable across Operating systems

1.8.2 Applications

1. GUI based desktop applications
2. Graphic design, image processing applications, Games, and Scientific/ computational Applications
3. Web frameworks and applications
4. Enterprise and Business applications
5. Operating Systems
6. Education
7. Database Access
8. Language Development
9. Prototyping
10. Software Development

1.8.3 Organizations using Python

1. Google(Components of Google spider and Search Engine)
2. Yahoo(Maps)
3. YouTube
4. Mozilla
5. Dropbox
6. Microsoft
7. Cisco
8. Spotify
9. Quora

2

Python Operators

2.1 Operators

Operators are those who perform some specific operation. Python has a wide variety of operators. The various python operators are categorized into:

1. Arithmetic operators
2. Comparison/relational operators
3. Assignment operators
4. Logical operators
5. Identity operators
6. Membership operators
7. Bitwise operator

2.1.1 Arithmetic Operators

Arithmetic operators are those that perform mathematical calculation. Arithmetic operators are

If a=4, b=2 then

Operators	Description	Example
+ (Addition)	Adds two or more numbers	a+b=6
-(Subtraction)	Subtracts two or more numbers	a-b
*(multiply)	Multiplies two or more numbers	a*b=8
/(division)	Divides two number	a/b=2
%(modulus)	Gives the remainder after dividing first number with second	a%b=0
**(exponent)	Return exponential (power)	a**b=16
//(floor division)	Divides two numbers but gives the quotient but removes the decimal place. But in case of Negative value it floors the number to far from zero.	a//b=2

2.1.2 Relational/Comparison Operator

Relational/comparison operators are those that perform comparison among operands. It gives either true or false based on the condition. Relational operators are:

a=4, b=2

Operator	Description	Example
>(Greater than)	Checks whether first number is greater than second	a>b return true
>=(Greater than equal to)	Checks whether first number is greater than equal to second number or not	a>=b return true
<(less than)	Checks whether first number is smaller than second	a<b return false
<=(less than equal to)	Checks whether first number is smaller than equal to second number	a<=b return false
==(Equal to)	Checks whether first number is equal to second number	a==b return false
!= (not equal to)	Checks whether first number is not equal to second number	a!=b return true

2.1.3 Assignment Operator

Assignment operator is used to assign a value to a variable

a=4,b=2,c=6

Operator	Description	Example
=	Assign values from right to left	c=a+b assigns value of a+b into c.
+= add & assign	It adds the right operand to left operand and assign the value to left operand	c+=a is equal to c=c+a
-= subtract & assign	It subtracts the right operand from left operand and assigns the value to left operand	c-=a is equal to c=c-a
*= multiply & assign	It multiplies the right operand with left operand and assign the value to left operand	c*=a is equal to c=c*a
/= divide & assign	It divides left operand with the right operand and assign the value to left operand	c/=a is equal to c=c/a
%=Modulus & assign	It divides left operand with the right operand and assign the remainder value to left operand	c%=a is equal to c=c%a

2.1.4 Logical Operators

Logical operators are used to combine conditional statements:

Operator: and, or, not

Example

```
a=5
b=6
c=7
((a>b)and(a>c))
```

2.1.5 Identity Operators

Identity operator in python is used to determine whether a value is of a certain class or type. For example, we can use the identity operators with built-in type() function to ensure that we are working with the specific variable type.

Operator	Description	Example
is	Returns true if both variables are the same object	x is y
is not	Returns true if both variable are not the same object	x is not y

Example

```
x=5
If(type(x) is int):
   print("correct")
      else:
          print("incorrect")
```

Example

```
x=5.2
If(type(x) is not int):
   print("correct")
      else:
          print("incorrect")
```

2.1.6 Membership Operator

Python provides two membership operators:

operator	Description
in	This returns true if the element is found otherwise false
not in	This return true if the element is not found otherwise true

Example

```
a=10
list=[1,2,3,4,5]
if(a in list)
  print("Yes a is present in the list.")
 else:
    print("no a is not present in the list")
```

Example

```
a=1
list=[1,2,3,4,5]
if(a in list)
  print("Yes a is present in the list.")
 else:
    print("no a is not present in the list")
```

2.1.7 Bitwise Operators

Bitwise operators are used to compare (binary) numbers:

Operator	Name	Description
&	AND	Sets each bit to 1 if both bits are 1
|	OR	Sets each bits to 1 if one of two bits is 1
^	XOR	Sets each bit to 1 if only one of two bits is 1
~	NOT	Inverts all the bits
<<	zero fill left shift	Shift left by pushing zeros in from the right and left the left-most bits fall off
>>	Signed right shift	Shift right by pushing copies of the leftmost bit in from the left, and let the rightmost bits fall off

Example

Let x=0000 0110

 y = 0000 1000

now x&y (bitwise &) =0000 0000

x|y (bitwise |) = 0000 1110

x^y (bitwise XOR) = 0000 1110

~x (x complement) = 1111 1001
x<<1 (1 step left shift) = 0000 1100
x>>1 (1 step right shift) = 0000 0011

2.2 Python Basic Program

1. Write a program to add two numbers.
2. Write a program to subtract two numbers.
3. Write a program to multiply two numbers.
4. Write a program to divide two numbers.
5. Write a program to perform addition/subtraction/multiplication/division in the same program.
6. Write a program to calculate:
   (a) Are of rectangle
   (b) Perimeter of rectangle
   (c) Area of square
   (d) Perimeter of square
   (e) Area of circle
   (f) Circumference of circle
7. Write a program to accept electricity unit consumption and calculate total price at the rate of 5 rs unit. Give a discount of 10% on all over bill.
8. Write a program to accept marks of 5 subjects and find total marks and percentage assuming full marks as 100 in each subject.
9. Write a program to swap values of two numbers.
10. Write a program to accept total sales amount and find the profit amount @5%.

Example 1: Write a program to perform addition/subtraction/multiplication/division in the same program.

```
a=int(input("enter 1st num:"))
b=int(input("enter 2nd num:"))
add=a+b
sub=a-b
mul=a*b
```

```
div=a/b
print("addition=",add)
print("subtraction=",sub)
print("multiplication=",mul)
print("division=",div)
```

Example 2: Write a program to calculate

(a) Are of rectangle
(b) Perimeter of rectangle
(c) Area of square
(d) Perimeter of square
(e) Area of circle
(f) Circumference of circle

```
# Python Program to find Area of a Rectangle
width = float(input('Please Enter the Width of a Rectangle: '))
height = float(input('Please Enter the Height of a Rectangle: '))
# calculate the area
Area = width * height
# calculate the Perimeter
Perimeter = 2 * (width + height)
print(Area)
print(Perimeter)
# Python Program to find Area Of Circle using Radius
PI = 3.14
radius = float(input(' Please Enter the radius of a circle: '))
area = PI * radius * radius
circumference = 2 * PI * radius
print(area)
print(circumference)
```

Example 3: Write a program to swap values of two numbers.

```
a=int(input("enter 1st num:"))
b=int(input("enter 2nd num:"))
c=a
a=b
b=c
print("value of a=",a)
print("value of b=",b)
```

3

Looping Statement

3.1 Control statement in python

Python statements are executed one by one in the same order as they appear in the program. But there may be some requirement when we want to execute the statements based upon a condition. Even there may be some situation where we want to execute a single statement or multiple statement (block of statement) "n" times till the condition is true. So in order to control the flow of execution of the program python provides us control statements.

There are two types of control statements:

(a) Selection statement

  (i) if

(b) Looping condition

  (i) While (ii) for

3.1.1 Selection Statement

Selection statements are used to select the statements based on a condition. In order words we can say that if there is some condition based upon which it is decided that whether a statement will be executed or not, then this is called selection statement. Python provides us "if" selection statement.

3.1.2 Looping Statement

Looping statements are used to execute a single statement or a block of statement (multiple statements) "N" times till the condition is true. Looping statement keeps on executing the statement till the given condition is true. Its stops working at the moment when the condition becomes false.

3.1.3 If Statement

If is a bi-directional conditional control statement that checks the condition and work according to that condition. A condition may have only two results:

either the condition is true the condition is false.

a. If condition :

   Statement 1

   Statement 2

   Statement n

b. If condition :

   Statement 1

   ----

   else:

   statement 1

   ----

c. If condition :

   Statement 1

   ----

   elif condition :

   statement 1

   ----

   else:

   statement 1

There may be some condition when we want to test for multiple conditions.
Syntax:

d. If condition :

   Statement 1

   ----

   elif condition :

   statement 1

```
-----------------
elif condition :
statement 1
-----------------
else:
statement 1
-----------------
```

Level 1 program

Example 1: write a program to check whether a number is odd/even.

Solution

```
 a=int(input("enter the number to check:")
if (a%2==0):
   print("the number is even.")
else:
  print("the number is odd.")
```

Example 2: Write a program to check whether an age is able to voting or not

Solution

```
a=int(input("enter your age:")
if (a>18):
   print("Eligible vote.")
else:
   print("Eligible not vote.")
```

Example 3: Write a program to find max between two numbers

Solution

```
a=int(input("enter 1st num:"))
b=int(input("enter 2nd num:"))
        if (a>b):
             print("max no.", a)
        else:
             print("max no.", b)
```

Example 4: Write a program to find max between three numbers

Solution

```
a=int(input("enter 1st num:"))
b=int(input("enter 2nd num:"))
c=int(input("enter 2nd num:"))
    if (a>b and a>c):
        print("max no.", a)
    elif (b>a and b>c):
        print("max no.", b)
    else:
        print("max no.", c)
```

Example 5: Write a program to check whether a given number is positive, negative or zero.

Solution

```
a=int(input("enter 1st num:"))
    if (a>0):
        print("positive no.")
    elif (a<0):
        print("negative no")
    else:
        print("zero.")
```

Example 6: Write a program to calculate total marks in 5 subjects (Full marks=100) as well as percentage of marked division as per the following condition:

Percentage>=80-Grade A
Percentage>=60-Grade B
Percentage>=40-Grade C
Percentage<40-Grade D

Solution

```
a=int(input("enter 1st num:"))
b=int(input("enter 2nd num:"))
c=int(input("enter 3rd  num:"))
d=int(input("enter 4rt num:"))
e=int(input("enter 5th num:"))
total = a+b+c+d+e
percent=(total/500)*100
print("Total Marks=", total,"Percentage", percent)
```

```
if (percent>=80):
        print("you have got grade A.")
  elif (percent>=60):
        print("you have got grade B.")
  elif (percent>=40):
        print("you have got grade C.")
else:
        print("you have got grade D.")
```

3.1.4 Looping Statement

Looping statement is a control statement which keeps on executing a single statement or a block of statements "N" times till the condition is true. Once the condition becomes false the execution is terminated.

Basically python provide the following looping statement:

1. While statement 2. For loop

Both the looping statement performs the same task. Only the difference is their syntax.

3.1.5 While Loop

While loop is a control statement which keeps on executing a single statement or a block of statements "N" times till the condition is true. Once the condition become false the execution is terminated.

Every looping statement has three parts:

a. Initialization

b. Condition

c. Increment/Decrement

If anyone statement among the above three statement is missing then the loop will not execute.

Initialization

This is the initialization of the counter variable using loop will be executed. In other words, we can say that there must be some value from where to start and this value is called initialization.

Condition

This is the condition up to which the loop will keep executing. Till this condition is true, the loop body will keep executing and till the given condition becomes false.

Increment/Decrement

To terminate a loop either the counter variable is increased or decrease by a specified value. This is called Increment/Decrement.

Program	Initialization	Condition	Increment/Decrement
Print 1 to 10	i=1	i<=10	I=i+1
Print 2 to 10	i=2	i<=10	I=i+2
Print 10 to 1	i=10	i>=10	I=i-1

Example: Write a program to print from 1 to 10.

```
i=1
while(i<=10):
    print(i)
i=i+1
```

Example: Write a program to print from 1 to n.

```
n=int(input("enter number upto which you want to print"))
i=1
while(i<=n):
    print(i)
i=i+1
```

Example:Write a program to print from 10 to 1.

```
i=10
while(i>=1):
    print(i)
i=i-1
```

Example: Write a program to print from n to 1.

```
N=int(input("enter number"))
while(n>=1):
    print(n)
     n=n-1
```

Example: Write a program to find sum from 1 to n

```
n=int(input("enter number upto which you want to print"))
i=1
sum=0
while(i<=n):
   sum=sum+i
    i=i+1
print("sum=sum",sum)
```

Example: Write a program to find sum of square from 1 to n

```
n=int(input("enter number upto which you want to print"))
i=1
sum=0
while(i<=n):
   sum=sum+(i*i)
    i=i+1
print("sum=sum",sum)
```

Example: Write a program to find sum of cubes from 1 to n

```
n=int(input("enter number upto which you want to print"))
i=1
sum=0
while(i<=n):
   sum=sum+(i*i*i)
    i=i+1
print("sum=sum",sum)
```

Example: Write a program to print only even numbers between 1 to n

```
n=int(input("enter number up to which you want to print"))
i=2
while(i<=n):
   print(i)
    i=i+2
```

Example: Write a program to print only even numbers between 1 to n

```
n=int(input("enter number up to which you want to print"))
i=1
while(i<=n):
    if i%2==0:
        print(i)
    i=i+1
```

Example: Write a program to find sum of even numbers from 1 to n

```
n=int(input("enter number up to which you want to print"))
i=2
sum=0
while(i<=n):
    sum=sum+i
    i=i+2
print("sum of even numbers=sum",sum)
```

Example: Write a program to find sum of first n even numbers.

```
n=int(input("enter number to find sum"))
i=1
sum=0
count=0
while(count<n):
    if(i%2==0):
        sum=sum+i
        count=count+1
    i=i+2
print("sum of even numbers=sum",sum)
```

Level 2 program

Example:Write a program to find sum of digits of a given number.

```
i=int(input("enter number to find sum of digits"))
sum=0
while(i>0):
    sum=sum+i%10
    i=i//10
print("sum of digits=sum",sum)
```

Example:Write a program to find sum of square of digits of a given number.

```
i=int(input("enter number to find sum of square of digits"))
sum=0
while(i>0):
    sum=sum+(i%10)*(i%10)
    i=i//10
print("sum of square of each digits=sum",sum)
```

Example: Write a program to find sum of cube of digits of a given number.

```
i=int(input("enter number to find sum of cube of digits"))
sum=0
while(i>0):
    sum=sum+(i%10)*(i%10)* (i%10)
    i=i//10
print("sum of cube of each digits=sum",sum)
```

Example:Write a program to check whether a given number is Armstrong or not.

```
i=int(input("enter number to check for armstrong"))
orig=i
sum=0
while(i>0):
    sum=sum+(i%10)*(i%10)* (i%10)
    i=i//10
if orig==sum:
    print("Number is armstrong")
else:
print("Number is not armstrong")
```

Example: Write a program to check whether a given number is Armstrong or not.

```
n=int(input("enter number to check for Armstrong:"))
i=n
count=0
while(i>0):  #count no of digits
  i=i//10
  count=count+1
sum=0
i=n
while(i>0):
    digit=i%10
    x=1
   producr=1
   while(x<=count):
      product=product*digit
      x=x+1
   sum=sum+product
```

```
    i=i//10
if(sum==n):
   print("Armstrong")
else:
    print("not Armstrong")
```

Example: Write a program to find product of digits of a given number.

```
i=int(input("enter number:"))
prod=1
while(i>0):
    prod=prod*(i%10)
    i=i//10
print("product of digits=",prod)
```

Example: Write a program to reverse a given number.

```
i=int(input("enter number:"))
rev=0
while(i>0):
    rev=(rev*10)+i%10
    i=i//10
print("reverse=",rev)
```

Example: Write a program to check a number is palindrome or not.

```
i=int(input("enter number:"))
rev=0
x=i
while(i>0):
    rev=(rev*10)+i%10
    i=i//10
if(x==rev):
    print("palindrome number")
else:
     print("Not palindrome number")
```

Example: Write a program to check a number is prime or not.

```
n=int(input("enter number:"))
count=0
i=1
while(i<=n):
    if(n%i==0):
        count=count+1
    i=i+1
```

```
if(count==2):
   print("prime number")
else:
      print("composite number")
```

Example: Write a program to print factorial of a given number.

```
i=int(input("enter number:"))
fac=1
while(i>0):
     fac=fac*i
     i=i-1
print("Factorial=",fac)
```

Example1: Write a program to print Fabonacci series up to a given number.

```
n=int(input("enter number:"))
x=0
y=1
z=0
while(z<=n):
     print(z)
     x=y
     y=z
     z=x+y
```

3.2 Nested loop

Example 1: Triangle shape programming

```
i=1
while(i<=5):
              j=1
              while(j<=i):
                     print("*",end="")
                     j=j+1
             print()
              i=i+1
```

Example2(1)

```
i=1
while(i<=5):
              j=1
```

```
        while(j<=i):
              print("i",end="")
              j=j+1
       print()
        i=i+1
```

Example3(1)

```
i=1
while(i<=5):
        j=1
        while(j<=i):
              print("j",end="")
              j=j+1
       print()
        i=i+1
```

Example : printing stars * in reverse angle triangle shape

```
i=1
while(i<=5):
        b=1
        while(b<=5-i):
              print(" _ ",end="")
              b=b+1
         j=1
         while(j<=i):
          print("*",end="")
         j=j+1
       print()
        i=i+1
```

Example 1: printing pyramid program

```
k=1
i=1
while(i<=5):
        b=1
        while(b<=5-i):
              print(" _ ",end="")
              b=b+1
         j=1
         while(j<=k):
                print("*",end="")
```

```
            j=j+1
        k=k+2
      print()
       i=i+1
```

Example 2(1)

```
k=1
i=1
while(i<=5):
        b=1
        while(b<=5-i):
              print(" ",end="")
              b=b+1
        j=1
        while(j<=k):
              print(k,end="")
              j=j+1
        k=k+2
      print()
       i=i+1
```

Example3(1)

```
k=1
i=1
while(i<=5):
        b=1
        while(b<=5-i):
              print("_",end="")
              b=b+1
        j=1
        while(j<=k):
              print(i,end="")
              j=j+1
        k=k+2
      print()
       i=i+1
```

Example: print opposite pyramid shape

```
n=int(input("enter no of row"))
i=1
While(n>0):
```

```
b=1
 while(b<i):
        print("_",end="")
         b=b+1
  j=1
 while(j<=(n*2)-i):
         print("*",end="")
         j=j+1
 print()
 n=n-1
  i=i+1
```

3.2.1. For Loops in Python

- A for loop is used for iterating over a sequence (that is either a list, a tuple, a dictionary, a set, or a string).
- This is less like the for keyword in other programming languages, and works more like an iterator method as found in other object-orientated programming languages.
- With the for loop we can execute a set of statements, once for each item in a list, tuple, set etc.

Example: write a program to print table of a given number

```
x=int(input("enter no to find table"))
for y in range(1,11):
      print(x*y)
```

4

Function in Python Programming

4.1 Introduction to Function in Python

Python Functions is a block of related statements designed to perform a computational, logical, or evaluative task. The idea is to put some commonly or repeatedly done tasks together and make a function so that instead of writing the same code again and again for different inputs, we can do the function calls to reuse code contained in it over and over again. Functions can be both built-in or user-defined.

Function means sub-program

1. Function definition
2. Function call

Example:

```
def message:     #function definition
    print("hello python")
message()          #function call
```

Example:

Find addition of two number using function.

```
def add(-,-,-): #-argument of function it means input value
```

Example:

```
def addition(a,b):  #function define
    c=a+b
    print("addition=",c)
addition(5,6)    #function call
```

Example:

```
def addition(a,b):  #function define
    c=a+b
    print("addition=",c)
```

```
a=int(input("enter 1st no")
b=int(input("enter 2nd no")
addition(a,b)     # function call
```

4.1.1 Function Without Argument Program

```
def add:
    a=int(input("enter 1st no"))
    b=int(input("enter 2nd  no"))
    c=a+b
   print("Addition=",c)
 add()
```

4.1.2 Function Parameters/Arguments in Python

This is the value which is supplied to the function operator on

<table>
<tr><th colspan="2">Comparison between</th></tr>
<tr><td>Without argument</td><td>With argument</td></tr>
<tr><td>Example:
def addition:
        a=int(input("enter 1st no")
        b=int(input("enter 2nd no")
        c=a+b
        print("addition=",c)
addition()</td><td>Example:
def addition(a,b):
        c=a+b
        print("addition=",c)
addition(5,6)</td></tr>
<tr><td>Example:
def oddeven:
      a=int(input("enter 1st no")
      if(a%2==0):
            print("even")
       else:
            print("odd")
oddeven()</td><td>Example:
def oddeven(a):
            if(a%2==0):
            print("even")
            else:
            print("odd")
oddeven(6)
#######################
def oddeven(a):
            if(a%2==0):
            print("even")
            else:
            print("odd")
m=int(input("enter no")
oddeven(m)</td></tr>
</table>

4.2 Function Used

1. No argument no return
2. With argument no return
3. No argument with return
4. With argument with return

4.2.1 No Argument No Return

```
def add:
    a=int(input("enter 1st no"))
    b=int(input("enter 2nd  no"))
    c=a+b
   print("Addition=",c)
 add()
```

4.2.2 With Argument No Return

```
def add(a,b):
   c=a+b
   print("Addition=",c)
      a=int(input("enter 1st no"))
 b=int(input("enter 2nd  no"))
 add(a,b)
```

4.2.3 No Argument With Return

```
def add:
    a=int(input("enter 1st no"))
    b=int(input("enter 2nd  no"))
    c=a+b
   return c
 x=add()
 print("Addition=",x)
```

4.2.4 With Argument With Return

```
def add(a,b):
   c=a+b
   return c
      a=int(input("enter 1st no"))
 b=int(input("enter 2nd  no"))
```

```
z=add(a,b)
print("Addition=",z)
```

4.3 Default Argument

Python has a different way of representing syntax and default values for function arguments. Default values indicate that the function argument will take that value if no argument value is passed during the function call. The default value is assigned by using the assignment(=) operator of the form keywordname=value.

Syntax

```
def add(a,b,c=5):
    ------
    -----------
add(5,6)
```

Example

```
def add(a,b,c=5):
    d=a+b+c
    print("addition="d)
add(5,6,7)
ouptput:18
```

Example

```
def add(a,b,c=5):
    d=a+b+c
    print("addition="d)
add(5,6)
output:16
```

Note:if given default argument value start then put continue otherwise error generate.

4.3.1 Fruit Function(Function Return Value)

Calling the function generates a return value, which we usually assign to a variable or use as part of expression

Example

```
def add:
    a=int(input("enter 1st no"))
    b=int(input("enter 2nd  no"))
```

```
    c=a+b
   return c
x=add()
print("Addition=",x)
```

4.3.2 Scope of The Variable(Global and Local Variable)

Global variable: A global variable is one which is not the part of any function. It can be used in any function being a global variable.

Local variable: A local variable is one which is the part of the a function and that's why it can be used only within the function

Example

```
def add(a,b): #a,b,c are local variable
   c=a+b
   print("Addition=",c)
 m=int(input("enter 1st no")) #m, n are global variable
 n=int(input("enter 2nd  no"))
add(m,n)
```

Example

```
def demo():
   a=5
  print("a="+a)
a=10
print("a="+a)
demo()
output:
a=5 #for local
a=10 #for global
```

Note: If local and global both are variable same

4.4 Break and Continue in Python

Break: terminate the loop, **continue:** loop terminates particular condition otherwise loop continue run.

4.4.1 Break Statement

The break statement takes care of terminating the loop in which it is used. If the break statement is used inside nested loops, the current loop is terminated, and the flow will continue with the code followed that comes after the loop.

The flow chart for the break statement is as follows:

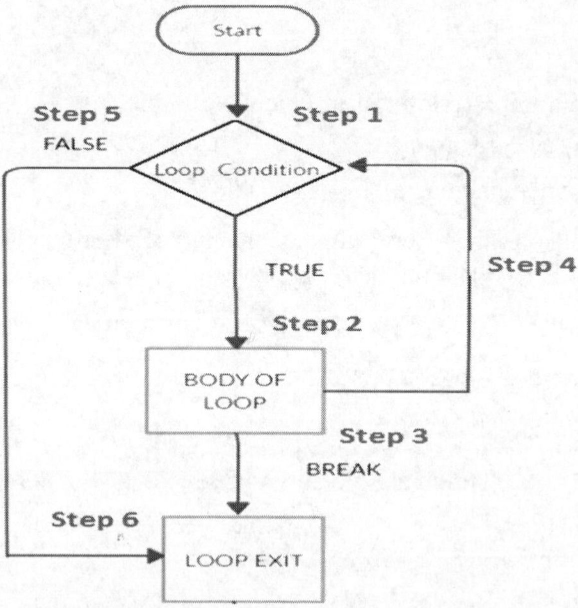

Fig. 4.1: Flow chart of break statment

The following are the steps involved in the flowchart.

Step 1: The loop execution starts.

Step 2: If the loop condition is true, it will execute step 2, wherein the body of the loop will get executed.

Step 3: If the loop's body has a break statement, the loop will exit and go to Step 6.

Step 4: After the loop condition is executed and done, it will proceed to the next iteration in Step 4.

Step 5: If the loop condition is false, it will exit the loop and go to Step 6.

Step 6: End of the loop.

Example

```
i=1
while(i<=5):
    if(i==3):
        break
```

```
    print(i)
    i=i+1
Output:1,2
```

4.4.2 Continue Statement

The continue statement skips the code that comes after it, and the control is passed back to the start for the next iteration.

The following are the steps involved in the flowchart.

Step 1: The loop execution starts.

Step 2: The execution of code inside the loop will be done. If there is a continued statement inside the loop, the control will go back to Step 4, i.e., the start of the loop for the next iteration.

Step 3: The execution of code inside the loop will be done.

Step 4: If there is a continue statement or the loop execution inside the body is done, it will call the next iteration.

Step 5: Once the loop execution is complete, the loop will exit and go to step 7.

Step 6: If the loop condition in step 1 fails, it will exit the loop and go to step 7.

Step 7: End of the loop.

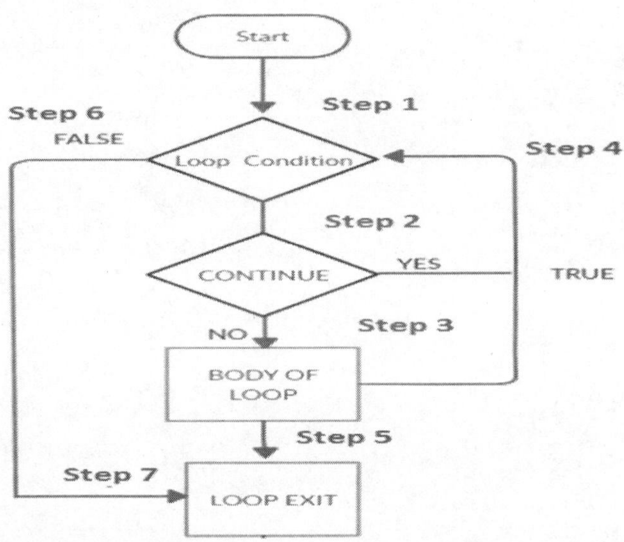

Fig. 4.2: Flow chart of continue statment

Example:

```
i=0
while(i<=5):
    i=i+1
    if(i==3):
        continue
    print(i)
    Output:1,2,4,5,6
```

5

String in Python Programming

5.1 String Statement

String in python is stored as individual characters i.e. indexed wise. The index by default starts with 0.

Forward indexing	0	1	2	3	4	5
string	p	y	t	h	o	n
Backward indexing	-6	-5	-4	-3	-2	-1

So, here P will be represented by str[0] or str[-6], y will be represented by str[1] or str[-5]

Note: strings are immutable and hence you cannot change the individual letters of string using assignment operator.

Example:

```
name=”shyam”
  Name[0]=”A”
Result error
```

Example:

```
name=”shyam”
print(name)
```

Example:

```
name=”shyam”
for i in name:
    print(i)
```

output

s
h
y
a
m

Example:

```
name="shyam"
for i in name:
    print(i,end="")
output: shyam
```

5.2 String Operators

1. **Concatenation operator (+):**The + operator concatenates two different string

   Example:

   ```
   x="Every"+"day"
      print(x)
   output:Everyday
   ```

2. **Replication operator (*):** The * operator requires two type of operands – a string and a number. It replicates the given string, to given number of times.

   Example:

   ```
   x=3*"hello"
   Print(x)
   Output: hellohellohello
   ```

3. **Membership operator(in/not in)**

Example

```
"a"in"ram"     output: true
"a"not in "ram"  output: false
```

4. **Comparison operators:**

   All relationa operators (>,<,>=,<=,==,!=) apply to strings also

Example

Comparison

“a”==”a”
“ram”==”ram”
“a”!=”ram”

Comparison always according ASCII code.

String slicing:

String slicing returns the characters falling between indices n and m:

String at n, n+1,n+2,….till m-1. The syntax is:

String[start:end:step_value]

Example

1.a=”hello word”
print(a[4:-2])
output:o wor
2.a=”hello word”
print(a[6:],a[:6])
output:word hello

Note:6: by default last tak print karega, :6 by default 0 se start karega

Str[6:10] last 9 tak print karega,

5.3 String Function

Python provides some built in functions. Some of the important are:

1. **len()** # This function returns the length of string

Exmple

a=”ram kumar”
print(len(a))

output: 9

2. **capitalize()** # This function returns a copy of the string with its first character capitalized.

Example:

```
a="shyam kumar"
print(a.capitalize())
output:Shyam kumar
```

Example:

```
a=input("enter you name:")
for i in range(0,len(a)):
    print(a[i])
```

Example: find reverse of a string

```
a=input("enter string:")
for i in range((len(a)-1),-1,-1):
Print(a[i],end="")
```

Example: find reverse of a string

```
a=input("enter string:")
Print(a[-1::-1])
```

Example: find total no vowels and consonant in given string

```
a=input("enter your name:")
vowel=0
cons=0
for i in range(0,len(a)):
    if(a[i]!=''):
        if(a[i]=="a" or a[i]=="e"or a[i] =="i" or a[i]=="o" or a[i]=="u"
                if(a[i]=="A" or a[i]=="E"or a[i] =="I" or a[i]=="O" or
a[i]=="U"]:
                vowel=vowel+1
        else:
            cons=cons+1
print("total vowels=",vowel)
print("total consonant=""cons)
```

3. **find()** # this function returns the lowest index in the string where the substring is found, it returns the index where it is found and if not found it returns -1

Example:

```
a="RAM IS GOING TO MARKET"
b="TO"
a.find(b,o,(len(a)-1))
output:13
```

Example: check a string is palindrome or not

```
a=input("enter string:")
b=a[-1::-1]
if(a==b):
  print("Palindrome string")
else:
   print("Not Palindrome string")
```

4. **isalnum()** # This return if the characters in the string are alphanumeric (alphabets or numbers) and there is at least one character otherwise it returns false

   Example:

```
a="ram123"
a.isalnum()
b="hello"
b.isalnum()
c="1234"
c.isalnum()
c=""
c.isalnum()
```

5. **isdigit()** # isalnum() # This return if all the characters in the string are digits and there is at least one digitotherwise it returns false

   Example:

```
a="ram123"
a.isdigit()
b="hell"
b.isdigit()
```

6. **isspace()** # This return true when there are only white spaces in the string and there is at least one character. Otherwise it returns false.

   Example:

```
a=" "
a.isspace() #output True
```

6

List in Python Programming

6.1 List Introduction

1. List is a collection of different values or different types of items.
2. Unlike array in c/c++/java a list is capable of storing different types of values under one roof.
3. The items in the list are separated with the comma (,) and enclosed with the square brackets [].
4. List provides us the facility to store multiple types of in a single unit.

Example:

a=["ram",1,"shyam",12.5]
b=[1,2,3,4]

0	1	2	3	Forward indexing
ram	10	shyam	12.5	
-4	-3	-2	-1	Backward indexing

a[0]=ram
a=["ram",1,"shyam",12.5]
print(a)
print(a[0])
ram

6.2 Python List Slicing

Same as string, we have the concept of list slicing in python

Examples:

a=["ram",10,"shyam",12.5]
a[0:]= [ram,10,shyam,12.5]
a[:]=[ram,10,shyam,12.5]
a[1:3]= [10,shyam]
a[:3]= [ram,10,shyam]

6.2.1 Updating List in Python

0	1	2	3	Forward indexing
ram	10	shyam	12.5	
-4	-3	-2	-1	Backward indexing

Example:

```
a=["ram",10,"shyam",12.5]
print(a[1])
a[1]="Ramesh"
output : a=[ram,10,shyam,12.5]
print(a[1])
output : a=[ram,Ramesh,shyam,12.5]
```

6.2.2 Deleting List in python

Example:

```
a=["ram",10,"shyam",12.5]
print(a[1])
del(a[1])
output : a=[ram,10,shyam,12.5]
print(a[1])
output : a=[ram, shyam,12.5]
```

6.2.3 Accessing List Elements to Perform Various Operations

0	1	2	3	Forward indexing
ram	10	shyam	12.5	
-4	-3	-2	-1	Backward indexing

Example:

```
a=["ram",10,"shyam",12.5]
for i in a:
    print(i)
```

1. len(list) # This method used to find total length of the list

Example

```
a=["ram",10,"shyam",12.5]
b=len(a)
print(b)
```

2. **max(list)** # This method used to find max value

Example

a=["ram",10,"shyam",12.5]
b=max(a)
print(b)

3. min(list) # This method used to find min value

Example

a=["ram",10,"shyam",12.5]
b=max(a)
print(b)

Case 1: what if we have a list of string and integer values and we want to use max function. In this case will produce an error message stating that string and integer value comparison is not possible.

Case2: what if string value comparison is there. In such case, it will be compared as a to z in ascending order.

Note: max or min compare for similar type elements in list

4. cmp(list1,list2) # This method is used to compare two list

Syntax:

cmp(list1,list2)

Returns: return 1 is list1 is greater than list2 return 0 if both the list are equal returns -1 is list2 is greater than list1

There are some certain cases for comparison for two lists

Case1:

a. If both the list contains integers, then the comparison is done from left to right. If we get a larger number at any particular index, that list becomes greater and further comparison is stopped.

b. If all the elements in both the list are similar and one list is larger is size the larger size list is greater.

c. And if both contain some value the lists are equal.

   List1=[2,4,6,8]

   List2=[2,4,6,9]

```
List3=[2,4,6,9,11]
List4=[2,4,6,8]
Print("comparing list1 and list2:")
Print(cmp(list1,list2)) #output -1
Print("comparing list2 and list3:")
Print(cmp(list2,list3)) #output -1
Print("comparing list1 and list4:")
Print(cmp(list1,list4)) #output 0
```

Case 2

a. When list contains multiple datatypes, in such case string is consider to be greater than integer

b. The comparison in case of multiple data types is done with the sorted case of comparison.

```
List1=[2,4,6,8]
List2=[2,4,6,'a']
List3=['a','b','c']
List4=['a','c','b']
Print("comparing list2 and list1:")
Print(cmp(list2,list1)) #output 1
Print("comparing list2 and list3:")
Print(cmp(list2,list3)) #output -1
Print("comparing list3 and list4:")
Print(cmp(list3,list4)) #output -1
```

5. **list.append(obj):**This method is used to append (add) a passed object at the end of the list. Note that the object is added to the last of the list.

   Syntax:

   ```
   list.append(obj)
   ```

Example

```
a=["ram","shyam","sita","gita"]
```

```
a.append("mita")
print(a)
output: ram,shyam,sita,gita,mita
```

Example

```
a=[]
for i in range(10):
    x=input("enter item to add in the list:")
    a.append(x)
print(a)
```

6. **list.count(obj):**This method is used to count the frequency of a given object.

Synatax:
list.count(obj)

Example

```
a=["ram","shyam","sita","gita"]
x=a.count("ram")
print("frequency=",x)
```

Example

```
a=[]
for i in range(10):
    x=input("enter item to add in the list:")
    a.append(x)
x=input("enter value whose frequency you want:")
f=a.count(x)
print("frequency of ",x,"is=",f)
```

Note: you have to specific that what type of data you are going to search for counting frequency. The type of input is the list determines the type of value whose frequency you want to get.

7. **list.index(obj):**This method is used to find the index of the object/element. This function returns the first index of the object/index if it is found otherwise it returns an exceptions showing that the element is not found.

Synatx: list.index(obj)

Example

```
a=["ram","shyam","sita","gita"]
x=a.count("ram")
print("index of ram=",x)
```

Example

```
a=[]
for i in range(5):
   x=input("enter item:")
   a.append(x)
x=input("enter value of index:")
f=a.index(x)
print("index = ",z)
```

8. **list.insert(index,obj)** :This method is used to inser an object/value at the given index.

Syntax: list.insert(index,object)

Example

```
a=[5,"ram",10]
a.insert(2,"shyam")
print(a)
output:5,ram,shyam,10
```

Example

```
a=[]
for i in range(5):
   x=input("enter item:")
   a.append(x)
print("orginal list is:",a)
index=input("enter index where you want to inser:")
value=input("enter value insert:")
a.insert(index,value)
print("list after insertion: ",a)
```

9. **list.remove(obj)** : This method is used to delete an object/value from te given list. Note that it removes/deletes the first occurrence of the list.

Syntax: list.remove(object)

Example

```
a=[5,"ram",10,"ravi",10]
a.remove(10)
print(a)
output: 5,ram,ravi,10
```

Example

```
a=[]
for i in range(5):
    x=input("enter item:")
    a.append(x)
print("orginal list is:",a)
val=input("enter value to remove:")
a.remove (val)
print("list after deletion: ",a)
```

10. **list.reverse()** : This method is used to reverse the elements present in the list in place. Here the word , in place means that the list gets reversed itself.

Syntax: list.reverse()

Example

```
a=[5,"ram",10,"ravi",10]
a.reverse()
print(a)
output:10,ravi,10,ram,5
```

Example

```
a=[]
for i in range(5):
    x=input("enter item:")
    a.append(x)
print("orginal list is:",a)
a.reverse()
print("list after reverse: ",a)
```

11. **list.sort() :** This method is used to sort the elements present in the list in either ascending order or in descending order. The list gets sorted itself. Note that the sorting in done with the similar data type, that means your list should have similar types of data otherwise it will show error. By default the sorting is done in the ascending order.

Syntax

1. List.sort(reverse="False") # ascending order,
2. List.sort(reverse="True") # descending order

Example

```
a=[]
for i in range(5):
    x=input("enter item:")
    a.append(x)
print("orginal list is:",a)
a.sort()
print("list after sort: ",a)
Note: if you write here like:
c=a.sort()
print(c)  #it is wrong because sort function ki value ko kahi copy
nahi kiya ja sakata hai.
```

12. list.pop(): this method is used to delete the last element from the list. Note that this function deletes the last elements from the list one by one.

Syntax: list.pop()

Example

```
a=[5,2,8,3,7]
a.pop()
print()
output:5,2,8,3
```

6.3 Basic Program List

1. Program to find sum of elements of the list
2. Program to count total number of odd and even numbers in the list.
3. Program to find sum of even numbers and product of odd number in list
4. Program to search a number in the list.
5. Program to count frequency of a given number.
6. Program to find max number in the list
7. Program to find min number in the list
8. Program to reverse the list itself.

9. Program to insert a number at given index in a list.
10. Program to remove a given number from the list.

Example: Program to find sum of elements of the list

```
a=[]
size=int(input("how many elements you want to enter:")
for i in range(size):
        val=int(input("enter number:"))
        a.append(val)
sum=0
for i in range(size):
    sum=sum+a[i]
print("sum of list elements=",sum)
```

Example: Program to count total number of odd and even numbers in the list.

```
a=[]
size=int(input("how many elements you want to enter:")
for i in range(size):
        val=int(input("enter number:"))
        a.append(val)
even=0
odd=0
for i in range(size):
      if(a[i]%2==0):
           even=even+1
      else:
      odd=odd+1
    sum=sum+a[i]
print("total even=",even, "total odd=",odd)
```

Example: Program to search a number in the list

```
a=[]
size=int(input("how many elements you want to enter:")
for i in range(size):
        val=int(input("enter number:"))
        a.append(val)
key=int(input("enter number of search:")
flag=0
for i in range(size):
      if(a[i]==key):
```

```
            flag=1
            pos=i+1
            break
    if(flag==1):
        print("enter found at:","pos","position.")
    else:
        print("element not found=")
```

Example: Program to count frequency of a given number

```
a=[]
size=int(input("enter size of list:")
for i in range(size):
    val=int(input("enter number:"))
    a.append(val)
key=int(input("enter number of frequency:")
count=0
for i in range(size):
    if(a[i]==key):
        count=count+1
    print("Frequency count=",count)
```

Example: Program to find max number in the list

```
a=[]
size=int(input("enter size of list:")
for i in range(size):
    val=int(input("enter number:"))
    a.append(val)
max=a[0]
for i in range(size):
    if(a[i]>max):
        max=a[i]
    print("max number=",max)
```

Example: Program to find min number in the list

```
a=[]
size=int(input("enter size of list:")
for i in range(size):
    val=int(input("enter number:"))
    a.append(val)
min=a[0]
```

```
for i in range(size):
    if(a[i]<min):
        min=a[i]
    print("min number=",min)
```

Example: Program to reverse the list itself.

```
a=[]
size=int(input("enter size of list:")
for i in range(size):
    val=int(input("enter number:"))
    a.append(val)
i=0
j=size-1
while(i<j):
    t=a[i]
    a[i]=a[j]
    a[j]=t
    i=i+1
    j=j-1
print("List after reverse=")
for i in range(size):
    print(a[i])
```

Example: Program to Find Second Max, Second Min

```
a=[]
size=int(input("enter size of list:")
for i in range(size):
    val=int(input("enter number:"))
    a.append(val)
minval=min(a)
print("min value in the list is:", minval)
a.remove(minval)
smin=min(a)
print("second min value in the list=",smin)
```

Max number

```
a=[]
size=int(input("enter size of list:")
for i in range(size):
    val=int(input("enter number:"))
    a.append(val)
```

```
a.sort()
print("max num:", a[size-1])
print("second max num:", a[size-2])
```

7

Tuple in Python Programming

7.1 Tuple Introduction

A tuple is a collection which is order and unchangeable. In python tuples are written with round brackets. Tuples in python are very similar to list which contains different types of elements with the following major differences.

It is declared as

tuple1=(1,2,3,"ram","shyam")

<table>
<tr><td>List</td><td>Tuple</td></tr>
<tr><td>List write in []</td><td>Tuple write in ()</td></tr>
<tr><td>List is mutable</td><td>Tuples are immutable</td></tr>
<tr><td>List occupies more memory spaces as compare that tuple</td><td>tuple occupies less memory spaces as compare that list</td></tr>
<tr><td colspan="2">Program implementation
import sys
list=[1,2,"ram","shyam","true","ravi"]
tuple=(1,2,"ram","shyam","true","ravi")
print("size of list=",sys.getsizeof(list))
print("size of tuple=",sys.getsizeof(tuple))</td></tr>
<tr><td>List takes more time to execute as compared to tuple</td><td>tuple takes less time to execute as compared to list</td></tr>
</table>

Program implementation

```
import timeit
listtime=timeit.timeit(stmt="[1,2,3,4,5,6,7,8,9]",number=1000000)
tupletime=timeit.timeit(stmt="(1,2,3,4,5,6,7,8,9)",number=1000000)
print("List takes time:", listtime)
print("Tuple takes time:", tupletime)
```

7.2 Program Implementation

Example:

```
import sys
list=[1,2,"ram","shyam","true","ravi"]
tuple=(1,2,"ram","shyam","true","ravi")
print("size of list=",sys.getsizeof(list))
print("size of tuple=",sys.getsizeof(tuple))
```

7.2.1 Insert Update & Deleting Tuple Elements

1. Using tuple display construct

   Tuple=() #empty tuple

   Tuple=(val1,val2,……)

2. Creating empty tuple

   Tuple1=tuple()

3. Creating single element tuple:

   Tuple=(2) #this will not be a tuple but as an integer class

   Tuple=(2,)#this will be a tuple a tuple class.

 # Here after the element you need to give, (comma).

Creating tuple from existing sequences: we can also use a built-in tuple type object(tuple()) to create tuples from sequence as per the syntax:

Tuple1=tuple(<sequence>)

Sequence can be of any type like strings. List and tuples

#Creating tuple from strings

t1=tuple('word')

Output:('w','o','r','l','d')

#creating tuple from list

list=[1,2,3,4,5]

tuple1=tuple(list)

output

tuple1=(1,2,3,4,5)

7.3 Different Types of Tuple

Ways to create tuple	The type of tuple
()	This is an empty tuple
(7,)	Tuple with one element
(1,2,3)	Tuple of integers
(1,2,3.4,5)	Tuple of numbers
('a','n','d')	Tuple of characters
('a',1,2,3.5,'ram')	Tuple of mixed data type
('ram','shyam','sita')	Tuple of string

7.4 Indexing & Slicing of Tuple in Python

7.4.1 Traversing Tuple

If every element excess one by one is called traversen tuple

Example:

```
tuple1=(1,2,3,4)
for t in tuple1:
    print(t)
```

Example:

```
tuple1=(1,2,3,4)
for i in range(len(tuple1)):
    print(tuple[i])
```

7.4.2 Joining Tuple

Example

```
tuple1=(1,2,3,4,5)
tuple2=(6,7,8)
tuple3=tuple1+tuple2
print(tuple3)
```

7.4.3 Repeating or Replicating Tuples

Example:

```
tuple1=(1,2,3)
tuple2=tuple1*3
print(tuple2)
output(1,2,3,1,2,3,1,2,3)
```

7.4.4 Slicing The Tuples

The syntax is

T=[start:stop:step]

Example:

```
tuple1=(10,11,12,13,14,15)
tuple2=tuple1[3:5]
print(tuple2)
```

Note: by default the step 1

Example :

```
tuple1=(10,11,12,13,14,15)
tuple2=tuple1[0:5:2]
print(tuple2)
output: (13, 14)
output: (10,12,14)
```

7.5 Tuple Function

1. **len()** # This method returns length of the tuple, i.e. the total counting of elements in the tuple.

Syntax: len(tuple)

Example:

```
employee=('ram', 'shyam', 101, 1.56)
len(employee)
```

2. **max()**

This method returns max value from the tuple.

Syntax: max(tuple)

3. **min()**

This method returns min value from the tuple.

Syntax: min(tuple)

4. **index()** # it returns the index of an existing element in the tuple.

Syntax:tuple name.index(item)

Example: a=(10,20,30,45,20,15)

a.index(30)

output:2

Note:it will return 1st value index

5. **count()**

count() method returns the frequency of given element.

Syntax: tuple.count(item)

Example:

a=(10,20,30,45,20,15)

a.count(30)

6. **tuple()**

This method is used as a constructor which is used to create tuples from different types of values.

Syantax: tuple(sequence)

Example:

1. Creating empty tuple
tuple()
2.Creating tuple from list
t=tuple([1,2,3])
output: (1,2,3)
3.Creating tuple from string
tuple1=tuple("xyz")
Output: ('a','b','c')
4.Creating tuple from key of dictionary
tuple1=tuple({1:'m',2:'n'})
tuple1
output: (1,2)

7.5.1 Creating, Updating, Deleting & Accessing Elements of Tuple in Python

- Change tuple values: Once a tuple is created, you cannot change its values because tuples are unchangeable or immutable.
- But there is another way to achieve this. You can convert the tuple into a list, change the list and convert the list back into a tuple.

Example

You need to convert the tuple into a list to be able to change it:

```
x=('apple','banana','cherry')
y=list(x)
y[1]='kiwi'
x=tuple(y)
print(x)
```

Check if item exists: To determine if a specified item is present in a tuple use the "in" keyword.

Example

```
tuple1=('ram','shyam','sita','gita')
if 'ram' in tuple1:
    print("yes the element is present in the tuple")
else:
   print("no element is not present in the tuple")
```

Add items

- Once a tuple is created, you cannot add items to it. Tuple are unchangeable.
- You cannot add items to a tuple

Example

```
tuple1=('apple','banana','cherry')
tuple1[3]='orange' #this will raise an error
print(tuple1)
```

Delete tuple elements:

Removing individual elements of the tuple is not possible. To remove entire tuple, just use the **del** statement.

Example

```
tuple1=('ram','shyam','sita','gita')
print(tuple1)
del(tuple1)
print("after deleting tuple")
print(tuple1)  # error show
```

8

Dictionary in Python Programming

8.1 Introduction to Dictionary in Python

A dictionary is a collection which is unordered changeable and index. In python dictionaries are written within curly brackets, and they have keys and values. Means the dictionary contains two things first is the key and the second is the value.

8.1.1 Create and Print a Dictionary

Example

```
dict1={'brand':'Suzuki','model':'dzire','year':2020}
print(dict1)
```

Accessing items: you can access the items of a dictionary by referring to its key name, inside square brackets.

Example

Accessing items: there is also a method called get() for the same task.

```
dict1={'brand':'Suzuki','model':'dzire','year':2020}
print(dict1)
y=dict1.get("model")
print(y)
```

8.1.2 Loop Through a Dictionary

Example

```
dict1={'brand':'Suzuki','model':'dzire','year':2020}
for x in dict1:
   print(x)
```

Note: this will print the index value

Example

```
dict1={'brand':'Suzuki','model':'dzire','year':2020}
for x in dict1:
   print(dict1[x])
```

Note: this will print the values.

We can use the values() function to return values of dictionary

Example:

```
dict1={'brand':'Suzuki','model':'dzire','year':2020}
for x in dict1.values():
    print(x)
```

8.1.3 Change Values in Dictionary

you can change the value of a specific item by referring to its key name:

Example:

```
dict1={'brand':'Suzuki','model':'dzire','year':2020}
dict1['year']=2018
output: ='brand':'Suzuki','model':'dzire','year':2018
```

8.1.4 Add Update Delete Elements in Python

Checking whether a key exists in the dictionary:

Example:

```
dict1={'brand':'Suzuki','model':'dzire','year':2020}
if 'model' in dict1:
   print("yes, 'model' is one of the keys in the dictionary")
else:
   print("NO, 'model' is not one of the keys in the dictionary")
```

8.1.5 Adding New Element in the Dictionary:

Example:

```
dict1={'brand':'Suzuki','model':'dzire','year':2020}
print(dict1)
dict1['color']='white'
print(dict1)
output:
{'brand':'Suzuki','model':'dzire','year':2020}
{'brand':'Suzuki','model':'dzire','year':2020,'color':'white'}
```

8.1.6 Dictionary & its Function Explained:

1. len() # this function is used to find length of the dictionary.

Example

```
dict1={'brand':'Suzuki','model':'dzire','year':2020}
x=len(dict1)
```

2. Removing items # pop() :this method removes the element with specified key name

Example

```
dict1={'brand':'Suzuki','model':'dzire','year':2020}
print(dict1)
dict1.pop('model')
print(dict1)
output:
{'brand':'Suzuki','model':'dzire','year':2020}
{'brand':'Suzuki' ,'year':2020}
```

3. popitem(): #this method removes the last element of the dictionary. But the in the version before 3.7 it was used to remove the

Example

```
dict1={'brand':'Suzuki','model':'dzire','year':2020}
print(dict1)
dict1.popitem()
print(dict1)
output:
{'brand':'Suzuki','model':'dzire','year':2020}
{'brand':'Suzuki','model':'dzire'}
```

8.1.7 Del Keyword

This keyword is also used to delete the dictionary itself.

Example

```
dict1={'brand':'Suzuki','model':'dzire','year':2020}
print(dict1)
del dict1
print(dict1)
output: error
```

8.1.8 Clear Keyword (Deletes all the Elements of Dictionary)

This keyword is also used to delete all the elements of the dictionary. Note that it just deletes the content of the dictionary so the dictionary is there but without an element.

Example

```
dict1={'brand':'Suzuki','model':'dzire','year':2020}
print(dict1)
dict1.clear()
print(dict1)
output:
{}
```

8.2 Dictionary Function in Dictionary

- 1.len()
- get()
- clear()
- pop()
- popitem()
- values()
- items()
- copy()
- fromkeys()
- keys()
- setdefault()
- update()

Copy()

Example

```
Dict1={'brand':'Suzuki','model':'dzire','year':2020}
x=dict1.copy()
print(x)
```

fromkeys() # The fromkeys() method returns a dictionary with the specified keys and the specified value.

Example

```
x={'firstkey','second key','thirdkey'}
y=0
x=dict1.fromkeys(x,y)
print(dict1)
```

output

setdefault() #

- The setdefault method returns the value of the item with the specified key.
- If the key does not exist, it inserts the key, with the specified value.

Example

```
dict1={'brand':'Suzuki','model':'dzire','year':2020}
x=dict1.setdefault('brand','toyota')
print(x)
output:
since 'brand' key is already present so it will return the value of this key.
suzuki
```

Example

```
dict1={'brand':'Suzuki','model':'dzire','year':2020}
x=dict1.setdefault('place','new delhi')
print(x)
output:
since 'place' key is not exist present in the dict1, it will insert this key with value and then the respective value "new delhi" will assigned to x and so "new delhi" will get printed.
```

Update()

The update() method inserts the specified items to the dictionary.

```
dict1={'brand':'Suzuki','model':'dzire','year':2020}
x=dict1.update('color','white')
print(x)
```

9

Numpy in Python Programming

9.1 Introduction Numpy

Numpy: is apython package which stands for "Numerical python".

This was created in 2005 by Travis Oliphant.

Using numpy we can perform the following functionalities:

1. Mathematical and logical calculation on array.
2. Fourier transforms and routines for shape manipulation.
3. It has built in functions for linear algebra random number generation.
4. Used for scientific calculations.
5. It is faster than python list.
6. It is fast because it is associated with c programming.

NumPy is often called as an alternate for MatLab (a programming platform designed specifically for engineers and scientists for data analysis, developing algorithms, create models and application etc.)

NumPy is used with packages like SciPy(Scientific Python) and Mat-Plotlib (plotting libray) and this makes it capable to replace MATLAB.

1. 1 Dimensional array is referred to as vector.
2. 2 Dimensional arrays are referred to as matrix.
3. 3 Dimensional arrays are referred to as Tensor.

9.2 Installing Numpy

1. Anaconda (https://www.anaconda.com/) is a free python distribution for SciPy stack. It is also available for linux and Mac.
2. Canopy, python(x,y) may also be used for the same but I will use Anaconda for this video tutorial series.
3. Download and install Anaconda and finish it.

4. After installation go to start menu and click on "Anaconda Navigator".
5. This comes with many options like Jupyter Notebook, Spyder, VS code etc.
6. Here we will use Jupyter notebook.

Work with Jupyter Notebook

Jupyter notebook has two mode:

1. Command mode-blue color
2. Edit mode-green color

Some shortcuts to remember:

1. To Run the program you have written press Ctrl+Enter.
2. To Run the command as well as insert a cell below-shift+enter
3. To insert a cell below just press "b".
4. To delete a cell-press ese button (to go to command mode as in edit mode you cannot delete the cell) and then "d" two times.

9.2.1 Creating Numpy Array (one dimensional)

Example

```
import numpy as np
a=[1,2,3,4,5]
myarr=np.array(a)
myarr
We can do it directly:
 import numpy as np
myarr=np.array(a[1,2,3,4,5])
myarr
```

9.2.2 Creating two Dimensional Array Using Numpy

Example

```
import numpy as np
a=[[1,2,3,4,5],[4,5,6],[7,8,9]]
myarr=np.array(a)
myarr
print("Total dimension=",myarr.ndim)
print("shape of array=",myarr.shape)
```

We can do it directly:

```
import numpy as np
myarr=np.array(a=[[1,2,3,4,5],[4,5,6],[7,8,9]])
myarr
```

9.3 Numpy Function

1. Zeros: This function creates an array (either one dimensional or multi-dimensional) and fill all the values with zero (0)

Example

```
import numpy as np
arr=np.zeros(5)
output:([0.,0.,0.,0.,0.])
Example:
import numpy as np
arr=np.zeros(2,3)
output: 0  0  0
        0  0  0
```

2. Zeros: This function creates an array (either one dimensional or multi-dimensional) and fill all the values with ones (1)

Example

```
import numpy as np
arr=np.ones(5)
output:([1.,1.,1.,1.,1.])
Example:
import numpy as np
arr=np.ones(2,3)
output: 1  1  1
        1  1  1
```

3. Eye function

This function creates an array with all the diagonal elements as 1 and rest as 0 (in a square matrix). In case of a non-square matrix the values are still 1 for diagonal (up to which it can draw diagonal) and rest are zero.

Example

```
import numpy as np
arr=np.eye(3)
```

output:

```
1 0 0
0 1 0
0 0 1
```

Example

```
import numpy as np
arr=np.eye(3,4)
```

output:

```
1 0 0 0
0 1 0 0
0 0 1 0
```

4. Diag function

This function creates a two dimensional array with all the diagonal elements as the given value and rest as 0 (in a square matrix).

Example

```
import numpy as np
arr=np.diag([1,5,3,7])
```

output:

```
1 0 0 0
0 5 0 0
0 0 3 7
```

5. Randint()

This function is used to generate a random number between a given range.

Syntax:

```
Rand(min,max,total_values)
```

Example:

```
Import numpy as np
arr=np.random.randint(1,10,3)
```

output:
may be any 3 number from 1 to 9.

6. rand()

This function is used to generate a random values between 0 to 1.

Syntax:

```
rand(number_of_values)

example:

import numpy as np

arr=np.random.rand(5)

output: may be any 5 number from 0 to 1.
```

9.3.1 Two Dimensional(2D)

Example:

```
import numpy as np
arr=np.random.rand(2,3)
output: may be any 5 number from 0 to 1.
```

7. This function is used to generate random values close to 0 (zero). This may return positive or negative number as well.

```
rand.(number_of_values)
```

Example

```
import numpy as np
arr=np.random.randn(3)
output: may be any 5 number from cantered to 0.
```

9.3.2 Indexing in 1 Dimensional Array

Example

```
import numpy as np
a[]
size=int(input("how may numbers?"))
for i in range(size):
   val=int(input("enter number"))
   a.append(val)
arr=np.array(a)
for i in range(arr.size):
    print(arr[i])
arr1=arr[2:4] #this will make a new array with element from array arr
```

from index 2 to 3.
print(arr1)

9.3.3 Reshaping of Array in Numpy in Python

Example

```
a=[1,2,3,4,5,6,7,8,9,10,11,12]
Arr=np.array(a)
Changing the shape
a.reshape(2,6)
a.reshape(3,4)
a.reshape(2,-1)
Example:
import numpy as np
arr=np.random.randint(1,50,12)
arr.shape
arr=arr.reshape(2,6)  # converting it to two dimensional array.
```

9.3.4 Seed Function in Python Programming

We know that randint() function generates random numbers. Every time we run the program, new set of random number is generated. But what if we want to fix seed, this generates fix set of random numbers.

Example

```
import numpy as np

np.random.seed(12)

arr=np.random.randint(1,100,10) # Now it will return the same random numbers till we change the integer as passed to seed at any computer.
```

9.3.5 Creating Two Dimensional Array in Python Programming

1. Indexing/slicing using double bracket notation

[0][0]	[0][1]	[0][2]
[1][0]	[1][1]	[1][2]
[2][0]	[2][1]	[2][2]

2. Indexing/slicing using single bracket notation

[0,0]	[0,1]	[0,2]
[1,0]	[1,1]	[1,2]
[2,0]	[2,1]	[2,2]

Example

```
import numpy as np
matrix=[]
row=int(input("enter number of row:"))
col=int(input("enter number of col:"))
for i in range(row):
  a=[]
  for j in range(col):
        val= row=int(input("enter number:"))
         a.append(val)
    matrix.append(a)
for i in range(row):
    for j in range(col):
        print(arr[i][j],end=" ")
    print()
print(type(arr))
```

9.3.6 Indexing of 2 Dimensional Array

First we will create a two dimensional arraya

a=np.array([[10,20,30],[40,50,60],[70,80,90]])

two method :

1. Indexing/slicing using double bracket notation
2. Indexing/slicing using single bracket notation

Syntax:

a[row range, col range]

Example: a[:2]

9.4 View Vs copy

- When we slice a sub-array from an array, it may be done by two ways.
- First is by making view and the second is using a copy of it.
- But there is some difference between both of them. If you make a view of an array, any changes made to the sub array will be replicated to the original array whereas if you make any copy, any changes made of copied sub array will not reflect on the original array.

Example

```
a=np.array([10,20,30,40,50,60,70,80])
slicing=a[3:6]
slicing[:]=0
print(a)
output: 10,20,30,0,0,0,70,80
```

Example

```
a=np.array([10,20,30,40,50,60,70,80])
slicing=a[3:6].copy()
slicing[:]=0
print(a)
output: 10,20,30,40,50,60,70,80
```

Note : this means the original array has not been updated.

9.5 Conditional Selection in Python Programming

9.5.1 Conditional Selection

Example

```
import numpy as np
arr=np.arange(1,16)
print(arr)
b=arr>10
print(b)
```

output

```
[ 1  2  3  4  5  6  7  8  9 10 11 12 13 14 15]
[False False False False False False False False False False  True  True
  True  True  True]
```

9.6 Operation on Numpy Array in Python Programming

Example

```
import numpy as np
arr=np.arange(1,5)
b=arr*2
b1=arr**2  # square every element
print(b)
output:[2,4,6,8]
```

Note: In numpy array divide by zero gives infinity and not any error.

9.6.1 Numpy Some More Function

```
import numpy as np

arr=np.array([10,20,30,40,50])

np.min(arr) # return the min number

np.max(arr) # return the max number

np.argmin(arr) # position of min number

np.argmax(arr) # position of max number

np.sqrt(arr) # square root of every number

np.sin(arr) # sin value of every number

np.cos(arr) # cos value of every number
```

linspace function returns values between a given range and with a same gab between consecutive elements.

```
import numpy as np

np.linspace(1,2,5)

output: 1.,1.25,1.5,1.75,2.
```

9.7 Creating 2D Array with Fixed Data Type

Example

```
import numpy as np
np.random.seed(122)
matrix=np.random.randint(1,21,9).reshape(3,3)
print(matrix)
np.sum(matrix) # find the sum of array
OR
matrix.sum()
np.min(matrix)  # find the min of matrix
np.max(matrix)  # find the max of matrix
```

Example

```
import numpy as np
np.random.seed(122)
matrix=np.random.randint(1,21,9).reshape(3,3)
```

```
print(matrix)
np.sum(matrix, axis=1) # find row wise sum
np.min(matrix, axis=1)  # find row wise win
np.max(matrix, axis=0)  # find col wise max
np.cumsum(matrix) #cumulative sum
np.cumsum(matrix, axis=0) #cumulative sum
```

Example

```
import numpy as np
np.random.seed(122)
matrix=np.random.randint(1,21,10)
print(matrix)
np.random.shuffle(arr) #shuffles the array elements
np.unique(arr) #display unique number of the array
np.unique(arr).size #count the unique count of the elements
```

Example

```
import numpy as np
np.random.seed(122)
matrix=np.random.randint(1,21,10)
print(matrix)
np.unique(arr, return_index=True, return_counts=true)
#returns three array
```

1. The array with unique values
2. The array with respective index values
3. The array with counting of frequency

9.7.1 Stacking 2D Array with Fixed Data Type

Example

```
import numpy as np
arr1=np.array([1,2,3,4])
arr2=np.array([5,6,7,8])
print(arr1)
print(arr2)
np.hstack((arr1,arr2))  #horizontally arranges the matrix
np.vstack((arr1,arr2)) #vertically arranges the matrix
```

Example

```
import numpy as np
np.random.seed(122)
arr1=np.random.randint(1,21,9).reshape(3,3)
arr2=np.random.randint(31,51,9).reshape(3,3)
print(arr1)
print(arr2)
np.hstack((arr1,arr2))  #horizontally arranges the matrix
np.vstack((arr1,arr2)) #vertically arranges the matrix
```

9.8 Question List

1. Write statement to import numpy
2. Create an array using numpy
3. Create an array of 10 random integers
4. Create an array of elements from 10-20
5. Create an array which contains value 5 times
6. Create a one dimensional array and covert that into 3*3 matrix
7. Create an array and then convert all the even numbers with o
8. Create a 2D array of size 3*3 but all the elements should be between 0 and 1.
9. Perform the following slicing:

   Input:
   ```
   1   2   3   4
   5   6   7   8
   9   10  11  12
   13  14  15  16
   ```

Output:

```
6   7
10  11
14  15
```

10. Concatenate 2D array horizontally and vertically.

Solution

Q 1.Write statement to import numpy

Answer

```
import numpy as np
```

Q 2. Create an array using numpy

Answer

```
import numpy as np
arr=np.array([1,2,3,4,5])
print(arr)
```

Q 3. Create an array of 10 random integers

Answer

```
import numpy as np
arr=np.random.randint(1,100,10)
print(arr)
```

Q 4. Create an array of elements from 10-20

Answer

```
import numpy as np
arr=np.arange(10,21)
print(arr)
```

Q 5.Create an array which contains value 5 times

Answer

```
import numpy as np
arr=np.ones()*5
print(arr)
```

Q 6. Create a one dimensional array and covert that into 3*3 matrix

Answer

```
import numpy as np
arr=np.arange(1,10).reshape(3,3)
print(arr)
```

Q 7. Create an array and then convert all the even numbers with o

Answer

```
import numpy as np

arr=np.arange(1,11)

arr[arr%2==0]=0

print(arr)
```

Q 8. Create a 2D array of size 3*3 but all the elements should be between 0 and 1.

Answer

```
import numpy as np

arr=np.random.rand(9).reshape(3,3)

print(arr)
```

Q 9. Perform the following slicing:

Input:

```
1   2   3   4
5   6   7   8
9   10  11  12
13  14  15  16
```

Output

```
6   7
10  11
14  15
```

Concatenate 2D array horizontally and vertically

Answer

```
import numpy as np

arr1=np.arange(1,17).reshape(4,4)

arr2=arr1[1:,1:3]

print(arr2)
```

Q10. Concatenate 2D array horizontally and vertically

Answer

```
import numpy as np
arr1=np.arange(1,10).reshape(3,3)
arr2= np.arange(10,19).reshape(3,3)
np.hstack((arr1,arr2))
```

Answer

```
import numpy as np
arr1=np.arange(1,10).reshape(3,3)
arr2= np.arange(10,19).reshape(3,3)
np.vstack((arr1,arr2))
```

9.9 Numpy vs List Difference

- Size-Numpy data structures take up less space.
- Performance-they have a need for speed and are faster than lists.
- Functionality-SciPy and NumPy have optimized functions such as linear algebra operations built in.

9.10 Pycharm Installation in Python IDE

Steps to Install PyCharm

Step 1: To download PyCharm, visit the official website of JetBrains: Download PyCharm.

Step 2: Click on the 'Download" button

Step 3: After that, you will see the below window with two options, **Professional** and **Community**

Step 4: Download the **Community** version

Note: If you are interested to work with the Professional version, then you can download the **Professional** version and avail a free trial.

9.11 Python Data Types

Data type defines the type of data a variable will store. In python, there is no strict rule for declaring variable. Data type is auto defined in python. In python, data type is set when you assign a value to a variable.

Example	Data type
a=”python programming”	str
a=20	int
a=20.5	float
a=1+5i	complex
a=[“apple”,”boy”,”cat”]	list
a=(“apple”,”boy”,”cat”)	tuple
a=range(5)	range
a={“name:”amit”,”age”:32}	dict
a={“apple”,”boy”,”cat”}	set
a=True/False	boolean

If we want to know the type of a variable we use “type” function

Example

```
x=5
Print(type(x))
```

9.11.1 Type Casting

Conversion of one data type into another type is called type casting. Casting in python is done using constructor functions.

Example

```
Int() # converts the argument into integer type
x=int(1) #x will be 1
y=int(2.8) #y will be 2
z=int(“3”) #z will be 3
```

9.11.2 Numpy Searching Arrays

we can also perform condition based searching using where() function. Consider an example if we want to get all the indexes where there are even numbers. The program would be.

Example

```
import numpy as np
a=np.array([1,2,3,4,5,6,7,8,9,10])
result=a.where(a%2==0)
print(result)
```

Searchsorted()

This method performs a binary search in the array, and returns the index where the specified value would be inserted to maintain the search order.

Example

```
import numpy as np
a=np.array([2,5,8,9,13])
result=a.searchsorted(a,7,side='right')
print(result)
```

10

Lambda Function in Python Programming

10.1 Lambda Function

Lambda Function or anonymous function in python programming

A lambda function can take any number of arguments, but can only have one expression.

Syntax:

Lambda arguments: expression only single line

The expression is executed and the result is returned.

Example

```
x=lambda a:a+10
Print(x(5))
```

Example

A lambda function can take any number of arguments.

```
x=lambda a,b:a*b
Print(x(5,6))
```

Example

```
x=lambda a,b,c:a+b+c
Print(x(5,6,2))
```

10.1.1 Filter Function with Lambda Function

The filter() function returns an iterator where the items are filter through a function to test if the item is accepted or not.

Example

```
ages=[5,12,17,18,24,32]
def myfunc(x):
```

```
  if x<18:
    return False
  else:
    return True
adults=list(filter(myfunc, ages))
for x in adults:
   print(x)
OR using lambda function
ages=[5,12,17,18,24,32]
adults=filter(lambda a:a>18, ages)
for x in adults:
  print(x)
```

Note: filter function use a function and list of values

Example

```
val=[5,12,17,18,24,32]
def myfunc(x):
  if x%2==0
    return True
  else:
    return False
adults=list(filter(myfunc, val))
for x in even:
   print(x)
OR using lambda function
val=[5,12,17,18,24,32]
even=filter(lambda a:a%2==0, val)
for x in even:
   print(x)
```

10.1.2 Map Filter Lambda Function in Python Programming

The map() function executes a specified function for each item in a iterable. The item is sent to the function as parameters.

```
ages=[5,12,17,18,24,32]
def myfunc(x):
  if x<18:
    return False
  else:
    return True
def myfunc1(x):
```

```
    return x*x
adults=filter(myfunc, ages)
for x in adults:
    print(x)
squares=map(myfunc1, adults)
for x in squares:
    print(x)
```

10.1.3 Map Function

Doing the same uding lambda function

Example

```
ages=[5,12,17,18,24,32]
adults=filter(lambda a:a>18, ages)
square=list(map(lambda a:a*a, adults)
print(square)
```

10.2 Reduce() Function

The reduce (fun, seq) function is used to apply a particular function passed in its argument to all of the list elements mentioned in the sequence passed along. This function is defined in "functools" module. At first step, first two elements of sequence are picked and the result is obtained.

Working

- At first step, first two elements of sequence are picked and result is obtained.
- Next step is to apply the same function to the previously attained result and the number just succeeding the second element and the result is again stored.
- This process continues till no more elements are left in the container. The final returned result is returned and printed on console.

Example

```
# python code to demonstrate working of reduce()
# importing functools for reduce()
import functools
def myfunc(a,b):
    return a+b
val=[1,2,3,4,5]
add=reduce(myfunc.val)
```

```
print("addition=",add)
```

OR using lambda function

```
import functools
val = [1, 3, 5, 6, 2]
add-reduce(lambda a,b, a+b, val)
# using reduce to compute sum of list
print("addition=: ", add)
```

Example

```
import functools
def myfunc(a,b):
   if a>b:
      return a
   else:
      return b
val=[1,2,3,4,5]
max=reduce(myfunc,val)
print("max=", max)
```

OR using lambda function

```
import functools
val=[1,2,3,4,5]
max=reduce(lambda a,b: a if a>b else b, val)
print("max=" max)
```

11

Pandas in Python Programming

11.1 Introduction

Pandas is an open-source Python Library providing high-performance data manipulation and analysis tool using its powerful data structures. The name Pandas is derived from the word Panel Data – an Econometrics from Multidimensional data.

In 2008, developer Wes McKinney started developing pandas when in need of high performance, flexible tool for analysis of data.

Prior to Pandas, Python was majorly used for data munging and preparation. It had very little contribution towards data analysis. Pandas solved this problem. Using Pandas, we can accomplish five typical steps in the processing and analysis of data, regardless of the origin of data — load, prepare, manipulate, model, and analyze.

Python with Pandas is used in a wide range of fields including academic and commercial domains including finance, economics, Statistics, analytics, etc.

11.1.1 Key Features of Pandas

- Fast and efficient DataFrame object with default and customized indexing.
- Tools for loading data into in-memory data objects from different file formats.
- Data alignment and integrated handling of missing data.
- Reshaping and pivoting of date sets.
- Label-based slicing, indexing and subsetting of large data sets.
- Columns from a data structure can be deleted or inserted.
- Group by data for aggregation and transformations.
- High performance merging and joining of data.
- Time Series functionality.

11.2 NumPy vs Pandas

NumPy array is used for the implementation of pandas data objects.

Python Pandas - Environment Setup

Standard Python distribution doesn't come bundled with Pandas module. A lightweight alternative is to install NumPy using popular Python package installer, **pip.**

pip install pandas

11.3 Introduction to Data Structures

Pandas deals with the following three data structures

- Series
- DataFrame
- Panel

These data structures are built on top of Numpy array, which means they are fast.

Dimension & Description

The best way to think of these data structures is that the higher dimensional data structure is a container of its lower dimensional data structure. For example, DataFrame is a container of Series, Panel is a container of DataFrame.

Data Structure	Dimensions	Description
Series	1	1D labeled homogeneous array, size immutable.
Data Frames	2	General 2D labeled, size-mutable tabular structure with potentially heterogeneously typed columns.
Panel	3	General 3D labeled, size-mutable array.

Building and handling two or more dimensional arrays is a tedious task, burden is placed on the user to consider the orientation of the data set when writing functions. But using Pandas data structures, the mental effort of the user is reduced.

For example, with tabular data (DataFrame) it is more semantically helpful to think of the **index** (the rows) and the **columns** rather than axis 0 and axis 1.

Mutability

All Pandas data structures are value mutable (can be changed) and except Series all are size mutable. Series is size immutable.

Note – DataFrame is widely used and one of the most important data structures. Panel is used much less.

11.3.1 Series

Series is a one-dimensional array like structure with homogeneous data. For example, the following series is a collection of integers 10, 23, 56,

10	23	56	17	52	61	73	90	26	72

Key Points

- Homogeneous data
- Size Immutable
- Values of Data Mutable

11.3.2 DataFrame

DataFrame is a two-dimensional array with heterogeneous data. For example,

Name	Age	Gender	Rating
steve	32	Male	3.45
lia	28	Female	4.6
vin	45	Male	3.9

The table represents the data of a sales team of an organization with their overall performance rating. The data is represented in rows and columns. Each column represents an attribute and each row represents a person.

11.3.3 Data Type of Columns

The data types of the four columns are as follows :

Colum	Type
Name	string
Age	integer
Gender	string
Rating	float

Key Points

- Heterogeneous data
- Size Mutable
- Data Mutable

11.3.4 Panel

Panel is a three-dimensional data structure with heterogeneous data. It is hard to represent the panel in graphical representation. But a panel can be illustrated as a container of DataFrame.

Key Points

- Heterogeneous data
- Size Mutable
- Data Mutable

11.4 Python Pandas Series

Series is a one-dimensional labeled array capable of holding data of any type (integer, string, float, python objects, etc.).

A pandas Series can be created using the following constructor

pandas.Series(data, index, dtype, copy)

The parameters of the constructor are as follows:

S.No.	Parameter & Description
1	data data takes various forms like ndarray, list, constants
2	index Index values must be unique and hashable, same length as data. Default **np.arrange(n)** if no index is passed.
3	Dtype dtype is for data type. If None, data type will be inferred
4	copy Copy data. Default False

A series can be created using various inputs like :

- Array
- Dict
- Scalar value or constant

11.4.1 Create an Empty Series

A basic series, which can be created is an Empty Series.

Example

```
#import the pandas library and aliasing as pd
import pandas as pd
s = pd.Series()
print(s)
```

Its **output** is as follows:

```
Series([], dtype: float64)
```

11.4.2 Create a Series From Ndarray

If data is an ndarray, then index passed must be of the same length. If no index is passed, then by default index will be range(n) where n is array length, i.e., [0,1,2,3.... range(len(array))-1].

Example

```
#import the pandas library and aliasing as pd
import pandas as pd
import numpy as np
data = np.array(['a','b','c','d'])
s = pd.Series(data)
print(s)
```

Its **output** is as follows:

```
0  a
1  b
2  c
3  d
dtype: object
```

We did not pass any index, so by default, it assigned the indexes ranging from 0 to **len(data)-1**, i.e., 0 to 3.

Example

```
#import the pandas library and aliasing as pd
import pandas as pd
import numpy as np
data = np.array(['a','b','c','d'])
s = pd.Series(data,index=[100,101,102,103])
print(s)
```

Its **output** is as follows

```
100  a
101  b
102  c
103  d
```

dtype: object

We passed the index values here. Now we can see the customized indexed values in the output.

11.5 Create a Series from Dictonary

A **dict** can be passed as input and if no index is specified, then the dictionary keys are taken in a sorted order to construct index. If **index** is passed, the values in data corresponding to the labels in the index will be pulled out.

Example

```
#import the pandas library and aliasing as pd
import pandas as pd
import numpy as np
data = {'a' : 0., 'b' : 1., 'c' : 2.}
s = pd.Series(data)
print(s)
```

Its **output** is as follows :

```
a 0.0
b 1.0
c 2.0
```

dtype: float64

Observe – Dictionary keys are used to construct index.

Example

```
#import the pandas library and aliasing as pd
import pandas as pd
import numpy as np
data = {'a' : 0., 'b' : 1., 'c' : 2.}
s = pd.Series(data,index=['b','c','d','a'])
print(s)
```

Its **output** is as follows :

```
b 1.0
c 2.0
d NaN
a 0.0
dtype: float64
```

Observe – Index order is persisted and the missing element is filled with NaN (Not a Number).

11.6 Create a Series from Scalar

If data is a scalar value, an index must be provided. The value will be repeated to match the length of **index**

```
#import the pandas library and aliasing as pd
import pandas as pd
import numpy as np
s = pd.Series(5, index=[0, 1, 2, 3])
print(s)
```

Its **output** is as follows:

```
0 5
1 5
2 5
3 5
dtype: int64
```

11.7 Accessing Data from Series with Position

Data in the series can be accessed similar to that in an **ndarray.**

Example

Retrieve the first element. As we already know, the counting starts from zero for the array, which means the first element is stored at zeroth position and so on.

```
import pandas as pd
s = pd.Series([1,2,3,4,5],index = ['a','b','c','d','e'])
#retrieve the first element
Print(s[0])
```

Its **output** is as follows:

Example

Retrieve the first three elements in the Series. If a : is inserted in front of it, all items from that index onwards will be extracted. If two parameters (with : between them) is used, items between the two indexes (not including the stop index)

```
import pandas as pd
s = pd.Series([1,2,3,4,5],index = ['a','b','c','d','e'])
#retrieve the first three element
Print(s[:3])
```

Its **output** is as follows:

```
a 1
b 2
c 3
dtype: int64
```

Example

Retrieve the last three elements.

```
import pandas as pd
s = pd.Series([1,2,3,4,5],index = ['a','b','c','d','e'])
#retrieve the last three element
Print(s[-3:])
```

Its **output** is as follows:

```
c 3
d 4
e 5
dtype: int64
```

11.8 Retrieve Data Using Label (Index)

A Series is like a fixed-size dict in that you can get and set values by index label.

Example

Retrieve a single element using index label value.

```
import pandas as pd
s = pd.Series([1,2,3,4,5],index = ['a','b','c','d','e'])
#retrieve a single element
Print(s['a'])
```

Its **output** is as follows :

Example

Retrieve multiple elements using a list of index label values.

```
import pandas as pd
s = pd.Series([1,2,3,4,5],index = ['a','b','c','d','e'])
#retrieve multiple elements
Print(s[['a','c','d']])
```

Its **output** is as follows :

```
a 1
c 3
d 4
dtype: int64
```

Example

If a label is not contained, an exception is raised.

```
import pandas as pd
s = pd.Series([1,2,3,4,5],index = ['a','b','c','d','e'])
#retrieve multiple elements
Print(s['f'])
```

Its **output** is as follows :

```
…
KeyError: 'f'
```

11.9 Python Pandas - DataFrame

A Data frame is a two-dimensional data structure, i.e., data is aligned in a tabular fashion in rows and columns.

Features of DataFrame

- Potentially columns are of different types
- Size – Mutable
- Labeled axes (rows and columns)
- Can Perform Arithmetic operations on rows and columns

Structure

Let us assume that we are creating a data frame with student's data.

Regd.No	Name	Marks%
1000	Shyam	78.2
1001	Raj	68.5
1002	Papu	56.8
1003	Sita	86.4
1004	Geeta	49.3

pandas.DataFrame

A pandas DataFrame can be created using the following constructor –

pandas.DataFrame(data, index, columns, dtype, copy)

The parameters of the constructor are as follows :

S.No.	Parameter & Description
1	data data takes various forms like ndarray, list, constants
2	index Index values must be unique and hashable, same length as data. Default **np.arrange(n)** if no index is passed.
3	columns For column labels, the optional default syntax is - np.arange(n). This is only true if no index is passed.
4	dtype dtype is for data type. If None, data type will be inferred
5	copy Copy data. Default False

11.9.1 Create DataFrame

A pandas DataFrame can be created using various inputs like:

- Lists
- Dict
- Series
- Numpy ndarrays
- Another DataFrame

In the subsequent sections of this chapter, we will see how to create a DataFrame using these inputs.

Create an Empty DataFrame

A basic DataFrame, which can be created is an Empty Dataframe.

Example

```
#import the pandas library and aliasing as pd
import pandas as pd
df = pd.DataFrame()
print df
```

Its **output** is as follows :

```
Empty DataFrame
Columns: []
Index: []
```

11.9.2 Create a DataFrame from Lists

The DataFrame can be created using a single list or a list of lists.

Example

```
import pandas as pd
data = [1,2,3,4,5]
df = pd.DataFrame(data)
print(df)
```

Its **output** is as follows :

```
0  1
1  2
2  3
3  4
4  5
```

Example

```
import pandas as pd
data = [['Alex',10],['Bob',12],['Clarke',13]]
df = pd.DataFrame(data,columns=['Name','Age'])
print(df)
```

Its **output** is as follows :

```
    Name    Age
0   Alex    10
1   Bob     12
2   Clarke  13
```

Example

```
import pandas as pd
data = [['Alex',10],['Bob',12],['Clarke',13]]
df = pd.DataFrame(data,columns=['Name','Age'],dtype=float)
print df
```

Its **output** is as follows:

```
    Name    Age
0   Alex    10.0
1   Bob     12.0
2   Clarke  13.0
```

Note – Observe, the **dtype** parameter changes the type of Age column to floating point.

11.9.3 Create a DataFrame from Dict of ndarrays / Lists

All the **ndarrays** must be of same length. If index is passed, then the length of the index should equal to the length of the arrays.

If no index is passed, then by default, index will be range(n), where **n** is the array length.

Example

```
import pandas as pd
data = {'Name':['Tom', 'Jack', 'Steve', 'Ricky'],'Age':[28,34,29,42]}
df = pd.DataFrame(data)
print(df)
```

Its **output** is as follows :

```
    Age   Name
0   28    Tom
1   34    Jack
2   29    Steve
3   42    Ricky
```

Note – Observe the values 0,1,2,3. They are the default index assigned to each using the function range(n).

Example

Let us now create an indexed DataFrame using arrays.

```
import pandas as pd
```

```
data = {'Name':['Tom', 'Jack', 'Steve', 'Ricky'],'Age':[28,34,29,42]}
df = pd.DataFrame(data, index=['rank1','rank2','rank3','rank4'])
print(df)
```

Its **output** is as follows :

```
        Age  Name
rank1   28    Tom
rank2   34   Jack
rank3   29  Steve
rank4   42  Ricky
```

Note – Observe, the **index** parameter assigns an index to each row.

10.9.4 Create a DataFrame from List of Dicts

List of Dictionaries can be passed as input data to create a DataFrame. The dictionary keys are by default taken as column names.

Example

The following example shows how to create a DataFrame by passing a list of dictionaries.

```
import pandas as pd
data = [{'a': 1, 'b': 2},{'a': 5, 'b': 10, 'c': 20}]
df = pd.DataFrame(data)
print(df)
```

Its **output** is as follows:

```
   a  b   c
0  1  2   NaN
1  5  10  20.0
```

Note – Observe, NaN (Not a Number) is appended in missing areas.

Example

The following example shows how to create a DataFrame by passing a list of dictionaries and the row indices.

```
import pandas as pd
data = [{'a': 1, 'b': 2},{'a': 5, 'b': 10, 'c': 20}]
df = pd.DataFrame(data, index=['first', 'second'])
print(df)
```

Its **output** is as follows:

```
        a  b   c
 first  1  2   NaN
second  5  10  20.0
```

Example

The following example shows how to create a DataFrame with a list of dictionaries, row indices, and column indices.

```
import pandas as pd
data = [{'a': 1, 'b': 2},{'a': 5, 'b': 10, 'c': 20}]
#With two column indices, values same as dictionary keys
df1 = pd.DataFrame(data, index=['first', 'second'], columns=['a', 'b'])
#With two column indices with one index with other name
df2 = pd.DataFrame(data, index=['first', 'second'], columns=['a', 'b1'])
print (df1)
print (df2)
```

Its **output** is as follows:

```
#df1 output
        a  b
first   1  2
second  5  10
#df2 output
        a  b1
first   1  NaN
second  5  NaN
```

Note − Observe, df2 DataFrame is created with a column index other than the dictionary key; thus, appended the NaN's in place. Whereas, df1 is created with column indices same as dictionary keys, so NaN's appended.

11.9.5 Create a DataFrame from Dict of Series

Dictionary of Series can be passed to form a DataFrame. The resultant index is the union of all the series indexes passed.

Example

```
import pandas as pd
d = {'one' : pd.Series([1, 2, 3], index=['a', 'b', 'c']),
  'two' : pd.Series([1, 2, 3, 4], index=['a', 'b', 'c', 'd'])}
df = pd.DataFrame(d)
print(df)
```

Its **output** is as follows :

```
   one  two
a  1.0  1
b  2.0  2
c  3.0  3
d  NaN  4
```

Note – Observe, for the series one, there is no label **'d'** passed, but in the result, for the **d** label, NaN is appended with NaN.

Let us now understand **column selection, addition**, and **deletion** through examples.

11.9.6 Column Selection

We will understand this by selecting a column from the DataFrame.

Example

```
import pandas as pd
d = {'one' : pd.Series([1, 2, 3], index=['a', 'b', 'c']),
  'two' : pd.Series([1, 2, 3, 4], index=['a', 'b', 'c', 'd'])}
df = pd.DataFrame(d)
print(df ['one'])
```

Its **output** is as follows :

```
a  1.0
b  2.0
c  3.0
d  NaN
```

Name: one, dtype: float64

11.9.7 Column Addition

We will understand this by adding a new column to an existing data frame.

Example

```
import pandas as pd
d = {'one' : pd.Series([1, 2, 3], index=['a', 'b', 'c']),
  'two' : pd.Series([1, 2, 3, 4], index=['a', 'b', 'c', 'd'])}
df = pd.DataFrame(d)
# Adding a new column to an existing DataFrame object with column label
by passing new series
print ("Adding a new column by passing as Series:")
```

```
df['three']=pd.Series([10,20,30],index=['a','b','c'])
print df
print ("Adding a new column using the existing columns in DataFrame:")
df['four']=df['one']+df['three']
print(df)
```

Its **output** is as follows:

```
Adding a new column by passing as Series:
   one  two  three
a  1.0    1   10.0
b  2.0    2   20.0
c  3.0    3   30.0
d  NaN    4   NaN

Adding a new column using the existing columns in DataFrame:

   one  two  three  four
a  1.0    1   10.0  11.0
b  2.0    2   20.0  22.0
c  3.0    3   30.0  33.0
d  NaN    4    NaN   NaN
```

11.9.8 Column Deletion

Columns can be deleted or popped; let us take an example to understand how.

Example

```
# Using the previous DataFrame, we will delete a column
# using del function
import pandas as pd
d = {'one' : pd.Series([1, 2, 3], index=['a', 'b', 'c']),
  'two' : pd.Series([1, 2, 3, 4], index=['a', 'b', 'c', 'd']),
  'three' : pd.Series([10,20,30], index=['a','b','c'])}
df = pd.DataFrame(d)
print ("Our dataframe is:")
print(df)
# using del function
print ("Deleting the first column using DEL function:")
del df['one']
print(df)
# using pop function
print ("Deleting another column using POP function:")
```

```
df.pop('two')
print(df)
```

Its **output** is as follows :

```
Our dataframe is:
     one    three  two
a    1.0    10.0   1
b    2.0    20.0   2
c    3.0    30.0   3
d    NaN    NaN    4
```

Deleting the first column using DEL function:

```
     three  two
a    10.0   1
b    20.0   2
c    30.0   3
d    NaN    4
```

Deleting another column using POP function:

```
   three
a  10.0
b  20.0
c  30.0
d  NaN
```

11.9.9 Row Selection, Addition, and Deletion

We will now understand row selection, addition and deletion through examples. Let us begin with the concept of selection.

11.9.10 Selection by Label

Rows can be selected by passing row label to a **loc** function.

Example

```
import pandas as pd
d = {'one' : pd.Series([1, 2, 3], index=['a', 'b', 'c']),
  'two' : pd.Series([1, 2, 3, 4], index=['a', 'b', 'c', 'd'])}
df = pd.DataFrame(d)
print(df.loc['b'])
```

Its **output** is as follows:

```
one 2.0
two 2.0
```

Name: b, dtype: float64

The result is a series with labels as column names of the DataFrame. And, the Name of the series is the label with which it is retrieved.

11.9.11 Selection by Integer Location

Rows can be selected by passing integer location to an **iloc** function.

Example

```
import pandas as pd
d = {‘one’ : pd.Series([1, 2, 3], index=[‘a’, ‘b’, ‘c’]),
  ‘two’ : pd.Series([1, 2, 3, 4], index=[‘a’, ‘b’, ‘c’, ‘d’])}
df = pd.DataFrame(d)
print(df.iloc[2])
```

Its **output** is as follows:

```
one   3.0
two   3.0
```

Name: c, dtype: float64

11.9.12 Slice Rows

Multiple rows can be selected using ‘ : ’ operator.

Example

```
import pandas as pd
d = {‘one’ : pd.Series([1, 2, 3], index=[‘a’, ‘b’, ‘c’]),
  ‘two’ : pd.Series([1, 2, 3, 4], index=[‘a’, ‘b’, ‘c’, ‘d’])}
df = pd.DataFrame(d)
print(df[2:4])
```

Its **output** is as follows :

```
    one   two
c   3.0    3
d   NaN    4
```

11.9.13 Addition of Rows

Add new rows to a DataFrame using the **append** function. This function will append the rows at the end.

Example

```
import pandas as pd
df = pd.DataFrame([[1, 2], [3, 4]], columns = ['a','b'])
df2 = pd.DataFrame([[5, 6], [7, 8]], columns = ['a','b'])
df = df.append(df2)
print(df)
```

Its **output** is as follows:

```
  a b
0 1 2
1 3 4
0 5 6
1 7 8
```

11.9.14 Deletion of Rows

Use index label to delete or drop rows from a DataFrame. If label is duplicated, then multiple rows will be dropped.

If you observe, in the above example, the labels are duplicate. Let us drop a label and will see how many rows will get dropped.

Example

```
import pandas as pd
df = pd.DataFrame([[1, 2], [3, 4]], columns = ['a','b'])
df2 = pd.DataFrame([[5, 6], [7, 8]], columns = ['a','b'])
df = df.append(df2)
# Drop rows with label 0
df = df.drop(0)
print(df)
```

Its **output** is as follows :

```
  a  b
1 3  4
1 7  8
```

11.10 Python Pandas - Panel

A **panel** is a 3D container of data. The term **Panel data** is derived from econometrics and is partially responsible for the name pandas – **pan(el)-da(ta)**-s.

The names for the 3 axes are intended to give some semantic meaning to describing operations involving panel data. They are –

- **items** – axis 0, each item corresponds to a DataFrame contained inside.
- **major_axis** – axis 1, it is the index (rows) of each of the DataFrames.
- **minor_axis** – axis 2, it is the columns of each of the DataFrames.

pandas.Panel()

A Panel can be created using the following constructor

pandas.Panel(data, items, major_axis, minor_axis, dtype, copy)

The parameters of the constructor are as follows :

Parameter	Description
data	Data takes various forms like ndarray, series, map, lists, dict, constants and also another DataFrame
items	axis=0
major_axis	axis=1
minor_axis	axis=2
dtype	Data type of each column
copy	Copy data. Default, **false**

11.10.1 Create Panel

A Panel can be created using multiple ways like:

- From ndarrays
- From dict of DataFrames

From 3D ndarray

Example

```
# creating an empty panel
import pandas as pd
import numpy as np
data = np.random.rand(2,4,5)
p = pd.Panel(data)
print(p)
```

Its **output** is as follows:

```
<class 'pandas.core.panel.Panel'>
Dimensions: 2 (items) x 4 (major_axis) x 5 (minor_axis)
Items axis: 0 to 1
Major_axis axis: 0 to 3
Minor_axis axis: 0 to 4
```

Note – Observe the dimensions of the empty panel and the above panel, all the objects are different.

From dict of DataFrame Objects

```
#creating an empty panel
Exmple:
import pandas as pd
import numpy as np
data = {'Item1' : pd.DataFrame(np.random.randn(4, 3)),
  'Item2' : pd.DataFrame(np.random.randn(4, 2))}
p = pd.Panel(data)
print(p)
```

Its **output** is as follows :

```
Dimensions: 2 (items) x 4 (major_axis) x 3 (minor_axis)
Items axis: Item1 to Item2
Major_axis axis: 0 to 3
Minor_axis axis: 0 to 2
```

11.11.2 Create an Empty Panel

An empty panel can be created using the Panel constructor as follows :

#creating an empty panel

Exmple:

```
import pandas as pd
p = pd.Panel()
print(p)
```

Its **output** is as follows –

```
<class 'pandas.core.panel.Panel'>
Dimensions: 0 (items) x 0 (major_axis) x 0 (minor_axis)
Items axis: None
Major_axis axis: None
Minor_axis axis: None
```

11.11.3 Selecting the Data from Panel

Select the data from the panel using

- Items
- Major_axis
- Minor_axis

Using Items

```
# creating an empty panel
import pandas as pd
import numpy as np
data = {'Item1' : pd.DataFrame(np.random.randn(4, 3)),
  'Item2' : pd.DataFrame(np.random.randn(4, 2))}
p = pd.Panel(data)
print(p['Item1'])
```

Its **output** is as follows :

```
         0          1          2
0  0.488224  -0.128637  0.930817
1  0.417497   0.896681  0.576657
2 -2.775266   0.571668  0.290082
3 -0.400538  -0.144234  1.110535
```

We have two items, and we retrieved item1. The result is a DataFrame with 4 rows and 3 columns, which are the **Major_axis** and **Minor_axis** dimensions.

Using major_axis

Data can be accessed using the method **panel.major_axis(index)**.

```
# creating an empty panel
Example
import pandas as pd
import numpy as np
data = {'Item1' : pd.DataFrame(np.random.randn(4, 3)),
  'Item2' : pd.DataFrame(np.random.randn(4, 2))}
p = pd.Panel(data)
```

```
print(p.major_xs(1))
```

Its **output** is as follows –

```
     Item1       Item2
0  0.417497   0.748412
1  0.896681  -0.557322
2  0.576657     NaN
```

Using minor_axis

Data can be accessed using the method **panel.minor_axis(index).**

```
# creating an empty panel
```

Example

```
import pandas as pd
import numpy as np
data = {'Item1' : pd.DataFrame(np.random.randn(4, 3)),
  'Item2' : pd.DataFrame(np.random.randn(4, 2))}
p = pd.Panel(data)
print(p.minor_xs(1))
```

Its **output** is as follows:

```
      Item1       Item2
0  -0.128637  -1.047032
1   0.896681  -0.557322
2   0.571668   0.431953
3  -0.144234   1.302466
```

12

Python Pandas Basic Functionality

12.1 Introduction Basic Functionality

By now, we learnt about the three Pandas DataStructures and how to create them. We will majorly focus on the DataFrame objects because of its importance in the real time data processing and also discuss a few other DataStructures.

12.2 Series Basic Functionality

S.No	Attribute or Method & Description
1	axes Returns a list of the row axis labels
2	dtype Returns the dtype of the object.
3	empty Returns True if series is empty.
4	ndim Returns the number of dimensions of the underlying data, by definition 1.
5	size Returns the number of elements in the underlying data.
6	values Returns the Series as ndarray.
7	head() Returns the first n rows
8	tail() Returns the last n rows.

Let us now create a Series and see all the above tabulated attributes operation

Example

```
import pandas as pd
import numpy as np
#Create a series with 100 random numbers
s = pd.Series(np.random.randn(4))
print(s)
```

Its **output** is as follows:

```
0  0.967853
1 -0.148368
2 -1.395906
3 -1.758394
dtype: float64
```

12.2.1 Axes

Returns the list of the labels of the series.

Example

```
import pandas as pd
import numpy as np
#Create a series with 100 random numbers
s = pd.Series(np.random.randn(4))
print ("The axes are:")
print s.axes
```

Its **output** is as follows :

The axes are:

[RangeIndex(start=0, stop=4, step=1)]

The above result is a compact format of a list of values from 0 to 5, i.e., [0,1,2,3,4].

12.2.2 Empty

Returns the Boolean value saying whether the Object is empty or not. True indicates that the object is empty.

Example

```
import pandas as pd
import numpy as np
#Create a series with 100 random numbers
s = pd.Series(np.random.randn(4))
print ("Is the Object empty?")
print s.empty
```

Its **output** is as follows:

Is the Object empty?

False

12.2.3 Ndim

Returns the number of dimensions of the object. By definition, a Series is a 1D data structure, so it returns

Example

```
import pandas as pd
import numpy as np
#Create a series with 4 random numbers
s = pd.Series(np.random.randn(4))
print(s)
print ("The dimensions of the object:")
print s.ndim
```

Its **output** is as follows:

```
0  0.175898
1  0.166197
2 -0.609712
3 -1.377000
dtype: float64
```

The dimensions of the object: 1

12.2.4 Size

Returns the size(length) of the series.

Example

```
import pandas as pd
import numpy as np
#Create a series with 4 random numbers
s = pd.Series(np.random.randn(2))
print s
print ("The size of the object:")
print s.size
```

Its **output** is as follows :

```
0  3.078058
1 -1.207803
dtype: float64
The size of the object:
2
```

12.2.5 Values

Returns the actual data in the series as an array.

Example

```
import pandas as pd
import numpy as np
#Create a series with 4 random numbers
s = pd.Series(np.random.randn(4))
print(s)
print ("The actual data series is:")
print s.values
```

Its **output** is as follows:

```
0  1.787373
1 -0.605159
2  0.180477
3 -0.140922
dtype: float64
```

The actual data series is:

[1.78737302 -0.60515881 0.18047664 -0.1409218]

12.2.6 Head & Tail

To view a small sample of a Series or the DataFrame object, use the head() and the tail() methods.

head() returns the first **n** rows(observe the index values). The default number of elements to display is five, but you may pass a custom number.

Example

```
import pandas as pd
import numpy as np
#Create a series with 4 random numbers
s = pd.Series(np.random.randn(4))
print ("The original series is:")
print(s)
print ("The first two rows of the data series:")
print s.head(2)
```

Its **output** is as follows :

```
The original series is:
0  0.720876
1 -0.765898
2  0.479221
3 -0.139547
dtype: float64
The first two rows of the data series:
0  0.720876
1 -0.765898
dtype: float64
```

tail() returns the last **n** rows(observe the index values). The default number of elements to display is five, but you may pass a custom number.

Example

```
import pandas as pd
import numpy as np
#Create a series with 4 random numbers
s = pd.Series(np.random.randn(4))
print ("The original series is:")
print(s)
print ("The last two rows of the data series:")
print s.tail(2)
```

Its **output** is as follows :

```
The original series is:
0 -0.655091
1 -0.881407
2 -0.608592
3 -2.341413
dtype: float64
The last two rows of the data series:
2 -0.608592
3 -2.341413
dtype: float64
```

12.3 DataFrame Basic Functionality

Let us now understand what DataFrame Basic Functionality is. The following tables lists down the important attributes or methods that help in DataFrame Basic Functionality.

S.No	Attribute or Method & Description
1	T Transposes rows and columns.
2	axes Returns a list with the row axis labels and column axis labels as the only members
3	dtypes Returns the dtypes in this object.
4	empty True if NDFrame is entirely empty [no items]; if any of the axes are of length 0.
5	ndim Number of axes / array dimensions.
6	shape Returns a tuple representing the dimensionality of the DataFrame.
7	size Number of elements in the NDFrame.
8	values Numpy representation of NDFrame.
9	head() Returns the first n rows.
10	tail() Returns last n rows.

Let us now create a DataFrame and see all how the above mentioned attributes operate.

12.3.1 Example

```
import pandas as pd
import numpy as np
#Create a Dictionary of series
d={'Name':pd.Series(['Tom','James','Ricky','Vin','Steve','Smith','Jack']),
  'Age':pd.Series([25,26,25,23,30,29,23]),
  'Rating':pd.Series([4.23,3.24,3.98,2.56,3.20,4.6,3.8])}
#Create a DataFrame
df = pd.DataFrame(d)
print ("Our data series is:")
print df
```

Its **output** is as follows:

```
Our data series is:
   Age  Name   Rating
0  25   Tom    4.23
1  26   James  3.24
2  25   Ricky  3.98
3  23   Vin    2.56
4  30   Steve  3.20
5  29   Smith  4.60
6  23   Jack   3.80
```

12.3.2 T (Transpose)

Returns the transpose of the DataFrame. The rows and columns will interchange.

Example

```
import pandas as pd
import numpy as np
# Create a Dictionary of series
d={'Name':pd.Series(['Tom','James','Ricky','Vin','Steve','Smith','Jack']),
  'Age':pd.Series([25,26,25,23,30,29,23]),
  'Rating':pd.Series([4.23,3.24,3.98,2.56,3.20,4.6,3.8])}
# Create a DataFrame
df = pd.DataFrame(d)
print ("The transpose of the data series is:")
print df.T
```

Its **output** is as follows:

```
The transpose of the data series is:
        0     1      2      3     4      5      6
Age     25    26     25     23    30     29     23
Name    Tom   James  Ricky  Vin   Steve  Smith  Jack
Rating  4.23  3.24   3.98   2.56  3.2    4.6    3.8
```

12.3.3 Axes

Returns the list of row axis labels and column axis labels.

Example

```
import pandas as pd
import numpy as np
```

```
#Create a Dictionary of series
d={'Name':pd.Series(['Tom','James','Ricky','Vin','Steve','Smith','Jack']),
  'Age':pd.Series([25,26,25,23,30,29,23]),
  'Rating':pd.Series([4.23,3.24,3.98,2.56,3.20,4.6,3.8])}
#Create a DataFrame
df = pd.DataFrame(d)
print ("Row axis labels and column axis labels are:")
print df.axes
```

Its **output** is as follows:

```
Row axis labels and column axis labels are:

[RangeIndex(start=0, stop=7, step=1), Index([u'Age', u'Name', u'Rating'],

dtype='object')]
```

12.3.4 Dtypes

Returns the data type of each column.

Example

```
import pandas as pd
import numpy as np
#Create a Dictionary of series
d={'Name':pd.Series(['Tom','James','Ricky','Vin','Steve','Smith','Jack']),
  'Age':pd.Series([25,26,25,23,30,29,23]),
  'Rating':pd.Series([4.23,3.24,3.98,2.56,3.20,4.6,3.8])}
#Create a DataFrame
df = pd.DataFrame(d)
print ("The data types of each column are:")
print df.dtypes
```

Its **output** is as follows:

```
The data types of each column are:
Age       int64
Name     object
Rating  float64
dtype:   object
```

12.3.5 Empty

Returns the Boolean value saying whether the Object is empty or not; True indicates that the object is empty.

Example

```
import pandas as pd
import numpy as np
#Create a Dictionary of series
d={'Name':pd.Series(['Tom','James','Ricky','Vin','Steve','Smith','Jack']),
  'Age':pd.Series([25,26,25,23,30,29,23]),
  'Rating':pd.Series([4.23,3.24,3.98,2.56,3.20,4.6,3.8])}
#Create a DataFrame
df = pd.DataFrame(d)
print ("Is the object empty?")
print df.empty
```

Its **output** is as follows:

Is the object empty?

False

12.3.6 Ndim

Returns the number of dimensions of the object. By definition, DataFrame is a 2D object.

Example

```
import pandas as pd
import numpy as np
#Create a Dictionary of series
d={'Name':pd.Series(['Tom','James','Ricky','Vin','Steve','Smith','Jack']),
  'Age':pd.Series([25,26,25,23,30,29,23]),
  'Rating':pd.Series([4.23,3.24,3.98,2.56,3.20,4.6,3.8])}
#Create a DataFrame
df = pd.DataFrame(d)
print ("Our object is:")
print df
print ("The dimension of the object is:")
print df.ndim
```

Its **output** is as follows:

Our object is:

```
   Age  Name   Rating
0  25   Tom     4.23
1  26   James   3.24
2  25   Ricky   3.98
```

```
3   23   Vin     2.56
4   30   Steve   3.20
5   29   Smith   4.60
6   23   Jack    3.80
The dimension of the object is:
2
```

12.3.7 Shape

Returns a tuple representing the dimensionality of the DataFrame. Tuple (a,b), where a represents the number of rows and **b** represents the number of columns.

Example

```
import pandas as pd
import numpy as np
#Create a Dictionary of series
d= {'Name':pd.Series(['Tom','James','Ricky','Vin','Steve','Smith','Jack']),
  'Age':pd.Series([25,26,25,23,30,29,23]),
  'Rating':pd.Series([4.23,3.24,3.98,2.56,3.20,4.6,3.8])}
#Create a DataFrame
df = pd.DataFrame(d)
print ("Our object is:")
print df
print ("The shape of the object is:")
print df.shape
```

Its **output** is as follows:

```
Our object is:
   Age  Name   Rating
0  25   Tom    4.23
1  26   James  3.24
2  25   Ricky  3.98
3  23   Vin    2.56
4  30   Steve  3.20
5  29   Smith  4.60
6  23   Jack   3.80
The shape of the object is:
(7, 3)
```

12.3.8 Size

Returns the number of elements in the DataFrame.

Example

```
import pandas as pd
import numpy as np
#Create a Dictionary of series
d={'Name':pd.Series(['Tom','James','Ricky','Vin','Steve','Smith','Jack']),
  'Age':pd.Series([25,26,25,23,30,29,23]),
  'Rating':pd.Series([4.23,3.24,3.98,2.56,3.20,4.6,3.8])}
#Create a DataFrame
df = pd.DataFrame(d)
print ("Our object is:")
print df
print ("The total number of elements in our object is:")
print df.size
```

Its **output** is as follows:

```
Our object is:
   Age  Name    Rating
0  25   Tom      4.23
1  26   James   3.24
2  25   Ricky   3.98
3  23   Vin     2.56
4  30   Steve   3.20
5  29   Smith   4.60
6  23   Jack     3.80
The total number of elements in our object is:
21
```

12.3.9 Values

Returns the actual data in the DataFrame as an **NDarray.**

Example

```
import pandas as pd
import numpy as np
#Create a Dictionary of series
d={'Name':pd.Series(['Tom','James','Ricky','Vin','Steve','Smith','Jack']),
  'Age':pd.Series([25,26,25,23,30,29,23]),
  'Rating':pd.Series([4.23,3.24,3.98,2.56,3.20,4.6,3.8])}
```

```
#Create a DataFrame
df = pd.DataFrame(d)
print ("Our object is:")
print df
print ("The actual data in our data frame is:")
print df.values
```

Its **output** is as follows:

```
Our object is:
   Age  Name   Rating
0  25   Tom     4.23
1  26   James   3.24
2  25   Ricky   3.98
3  23   Vin     2.56
4  30   Steve   3.20
5  29   Smith   4.60
6  23   Jack    3.80
```

The actual data in our data frame is:

```
[[25 'Tom' 4.23]
[26 'James' 3.24]
[25 'Ricky' 3.98]
[23 'Vin' 2.56]
[30 'Steve' 3.2]
[29 'Smith' 4.6]
[23 'Jack' 3.8]]
```

12.3.10 Head & Tail

To view a small sample of a DataFrame object, use the **head()** and tail() methods. **head()** returns the first **n** rows (observe the index values). The default number of elements to display is five, but you may pass a custom number.

Example

```
import pandas as pd
import numpy as np
#Create a Dictionary of series
d={'Name':pd.Series(['Tom','James','Ricky','Vin','Steve','Smith','Jack']),
  'Age':pd.Series([25,26,25,23,30,29,23]),
  'Rating':pd.Series([4.23,3.24,3.98,2.56,3.20,4.6,3.8])}
#Create a DataFrame
```

```
df = pd.DataFrame(d)
print ("Our data frame is:")
print df
print ("The first two rows of the data frame is:")
print df.head(2)
```

Its **output** is as follows:

```
Our data frame is:
   Age  Name   Rating
0  25   Tom    4.23
1  26   James  3.24
2  25   Ricky  3.98
3  23   Vin    2.56
4  30   Steve  3.20
5  29   Smith  4.60
6  23   Jack   3.80
```

```
The first two rows of the data frame is:

   Age  Name   Rating
0  25   Tom    4.23
1  26   James  3.24
```

tail() returns the last **n** rows (observe the index values). The default number of elements to display is five, but you may pass a custom number.

Example

```
import pandas as pd
import numpy as np
#Create a Dictionary of series
d={'Name':pd.Series(['Tom','James','Ricky','Vin','Steve','Smith','Jack']),
  'Age':pd.Series([25,26,25,23,30,29,23]),
  'Rating':pd.Series([4.23,3.24,3.98,2.56,3.20,4.6,3.8])}
#Create a DataFrame
df = pd.DataFrame(d)
print ("Our data frame is:")
print df
print ("The last two rows of the data frame is:")
print df.tail(2)
```

Its **output** is as follows :

```
Our data frame is:
   Age  Name   Rating
0  25   Tom    4.23
1  26   James  3.24
2  25   Ricky  3.98
3  23   Vin    2.56
4  30   Steve  3.20
5  29   Smith  4.60
6  23   Jack   3.80
The last two rows of the data frame is:
   Age  Name   Rating
5  29   Smith  4.6
6  23   Jack   3.8
```

13

Python Pandas Statistical Functions

13.1 Statistical Functions

Statistical methods help in the understanding and analyzing the behavior of data. We will now learn a few statistical functions, which we can apply on Pandas objects.

Percent_change

Series, DatFrames and Panel, all have the function **pct_change()**. This function compares every element with its prior element and computes the change percentage.

Example

```
import pandas as pd
import numpy as np
s = pd.Series([1,2,3,4,5,4])
print s.pct_change()
df = pd.DataFrame(np.random.randn(5, 2))
print(df.pct_change())
```

Its **output** is as follows:

```
0       NaN
1  1.000000
2  0.500000
3  0.333333
4  0.250000
5 -0.200000
dtype: float64

           0          1
0        NaN        NaN
1 -15.151902   0.174730
2  -0.746374  -1.449088
```

```
3 -3.582229    -3.165836
4  15.601150   -1.860434
```

By default, the **pct_change()** operates on columns; if you want to apply the same row wise, then use **axis=1()** argument.

13.1.1 Covariance

Covariance is applied on series data. The Series object has a method cov to compute covariance between series objects. NA will be excluded automatically.

Cov Series

Example

```
import pandas as pd
import numpy as np
s1 = pd.Series(np.random.randn(10))
s2 = pd.Series(np.random.randn(10))
print(s1.cov(s2))
```

Its **output** is as follows:

```
-0.12978405324
```

Covariance method when applied on a DataFrame, computes **cov** between all the columns.

Example

```
import pandas as pd
import numpy as np
frame = pd.DataFrame(np.random.randn(10, 5), columns=['a', 'b', 'c', 'd',
'e'])
print frame['a'].cov(frame['b'])
print(frame.cov())
```

Its **output** is as follows:

```
-0.58312921152741437
         a          b          c          d          e
a  1.780628  -0.583129  -0.185575   0.003679  -0.136558
b -0.583129   1.297011   0.136530  -0.523719   0.251064
c -0.185575   0.136530   0.915227  -0.053881  -0.058926
d  0.003679  -0.523719  -0.053881   1.521426  -0.487694
e -0.136558   0.251064  -0.058926  -0.487694   0.960761
```

Note – Observe the **cov** between **a** and **b** column in the first statement and the same is the value returned by cov on DataFrame.

13.1.2 Correlation

Correlation shows the linear relationship between any two array of values (series). There are multiple methods to compute the correlation like pearson(default), spearman and kendall.

Example

```
import pandas as pd
import numpy as np
frame = pd.DataFrame(np.random.randn(10, 5), columns=['a', 'b', 'c', 'd',
'e'])
print frame['a'].corr(frame['b'])
print(frame.corr())
```

Its **output** is as follows:

```
-0.383712785514
          a         b         c         d         e
a  1.000000 -0.383713 -0.145368  0.002235 -0.104405
b -0.383713  1.000000  0.125311 -0.372821  0.224908
c -0.145368  0.125311  1.000000 -0.045661 -0.062840
d  0.002235 -0.372821 -0.045661  1.000000 -0.403380
e -0.104405  0.224908 -0.062840 -0.403380  1.000000
```

If any non-numeric column is present in the DataFrame, it is excluded automatically.

13.1.3 Data Ranking

Data Ranking produces ranking for each element in the array of elements. In case of ties, assigns the mean rank.

Example

```
import pandas as pd
import numpy as np
s = pd.Series(np.random.np.random.randn(5), index=list('abcde'))
s['d'] = s['b'] # so there's a tie
print(s.rank())
```

Its **output** is as follows –

```
a 1.0
b 3.5
c 2.0
d 3.5
```

e 5.0
dtype: float64

Rank optionally takes a parameter ascending which by default is true; when false, data is reverse-ranked, with larger values assigned a smaller rank.

Rank supports different tie-breaking methods, specified with the method parameter –

- **average** – average rank of tied group
- **min** – lowest rank in the group
- **max** – highest rank in the group
- **first** – ranks assigned in the order they appear in the array

14

Python Pandas Visualization

14.1 Basic Plotting: plot

This functionality on Series and DataFrame is just a simple wrapper around the **matplotlib libraries plot()** method.

Example

```
import pandas as pd

import numpy as np

df = pd.DataFrame(np.random.randn(10,4),index=pd.date_range('1/1/2000',
  periods=10), columns=list('ABCD'))

df.plot()
```

Its **output** is as follows:

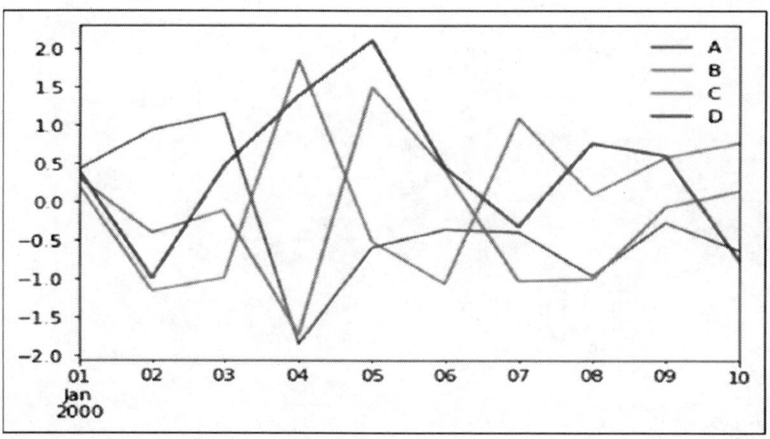

Fig. 14.1: Basic Plotting

If the index consists of dates, it calls **gct().autofmt_xdate()** to format the x-axis as shown in the above illustration.

We can plot one column versus another using the **x** and **y** keywords.

Plotting methods allow a handful of plot styles other than the default line plot. These methods can be provided as the kind keyword argument to **plot()**. These include –

- bar or barh for bar plots
- hist for histogram
- box for boxplot
- 'area' for area plots
- 'scatter' for scatter plots

14.1.1 Bar Plot

Let us now see what a Bar Plot is by creating one. A bar plot can be created in the following way.

Example

```
import pandas as pd
import numpy as np
df = pd.DataFrame(np.random.rand(10,4),columns=['a','b','c','d')
df.plot.bar()
```

Its **output** is as follows:

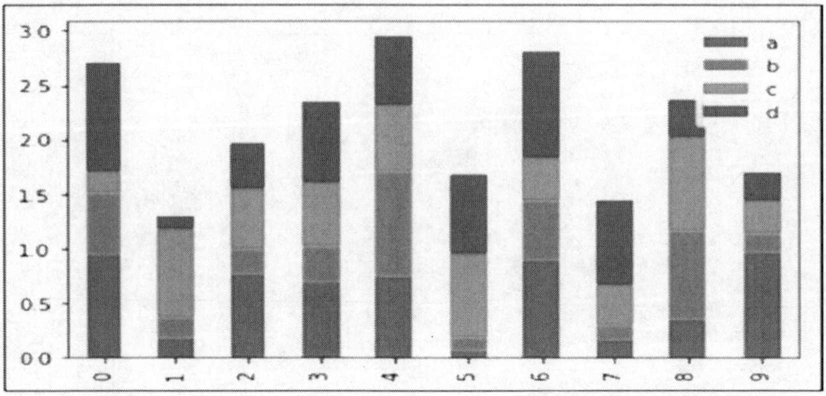

Fig. 14.2: Bar plot

To produce a stacked bar plot, **pass stacked=True**

Example

```
import pandas as pd
df = pd.DataFrame(np.random.rand(10,4),columns=['a','b','c','d')
df.plot.bar(stacked=True)
```

Its **output** is as follows

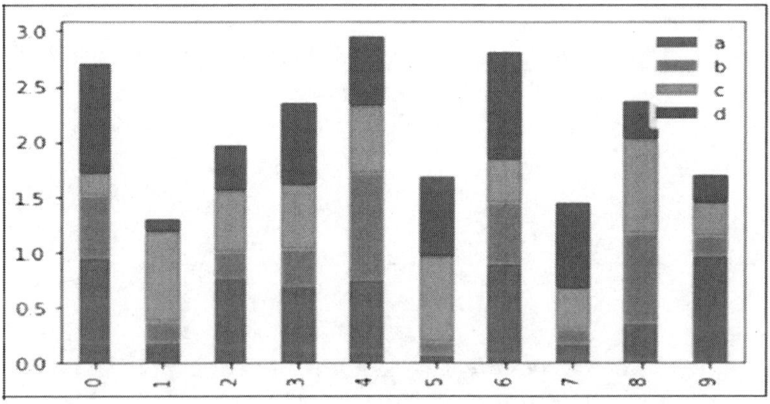

Fig. 14.3: Bar plot

To get horizontal bar plots, use the **barh** method

Example

```
import pandas as pd
import numpy as np
df = pd.DataFrame(np.random.rand(10,4),columns=['a','b','c','d')
df.plot.barh(stacked=True)
```

Its **output** is as follows

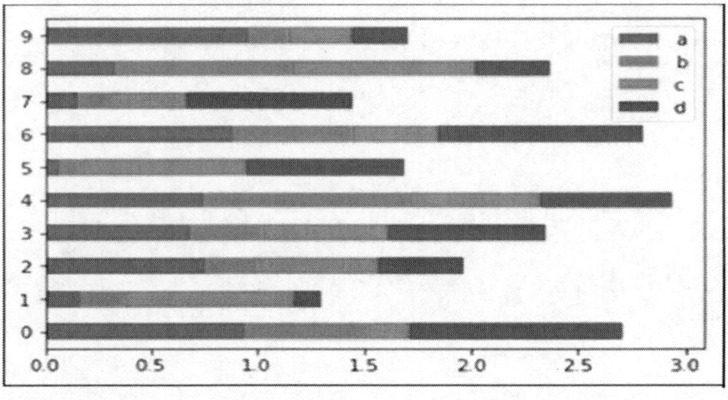

Fig. 14.4: Bar plot

14.1.2 Histograms

Histograms can be plotted using the **plot.hist()** method. We can specify number of bins.

Example

```
import pandas as pd
import numpy as np
df = pd. Data Frame ({'a':np.random.randn(1000)+1,'b':np.random.randn
(1000),'c':
np.random.randn(1000) - 1}, columns=['a', 'b', 'c'])
df.plot.hist(bins=20)
```

Its **output** is as follows:

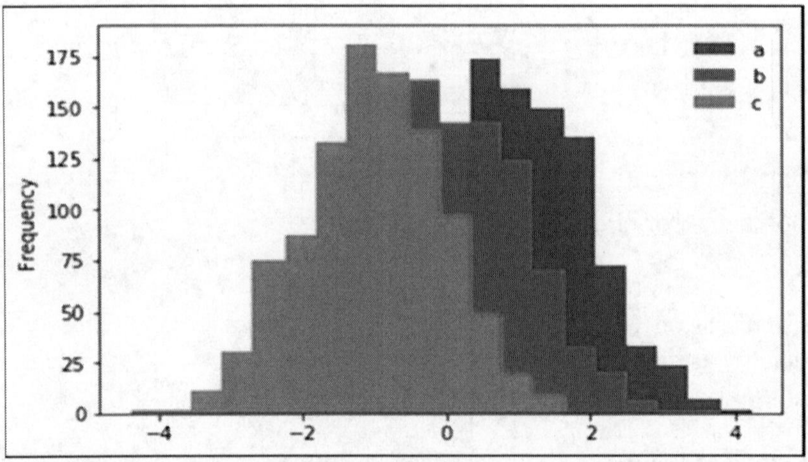

Fig. 14.5: Histrogram plot

To plot different histograms for each column, use the following code

Example

```
import pandas as pd
import numpy as np
df=pd.DataFrame({'a':np.random.randn(1000)+1,'b':np.random.
randn(1000),'c':
np.random.randn(1000) - 1}, columns=['a', 'b', 'c'])
df.diff.hist(bins=20)
```

Its **output** is as follows:

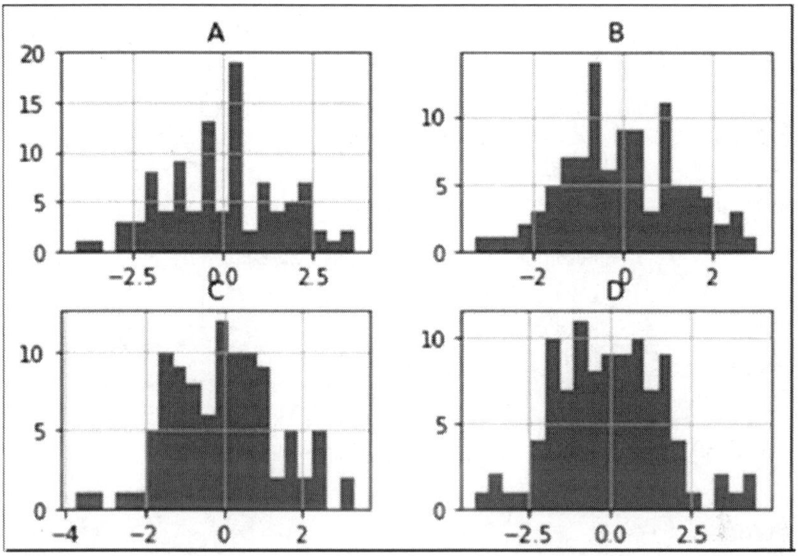

Fig. 14.6: Histrogram plot

14.1.3 Box Plots

Boxplot can be drawn calling **Series.box.plot()** and **DataFrame.box.plot()**, or **DataFrame.boxplot()** to visualize the distribution of values within each column.

For instance, here is a boxplot representing five trials of 10 observations of a uniform random variable on [0,1).

Example

```
import pandas as pd
import numpy as np
df = pd.DataFrame(np.random.rand(10, 5), columns=['A', 'B', 'C', 'D', 'E'])
df.plot.box()
```

Its **output** is as follows

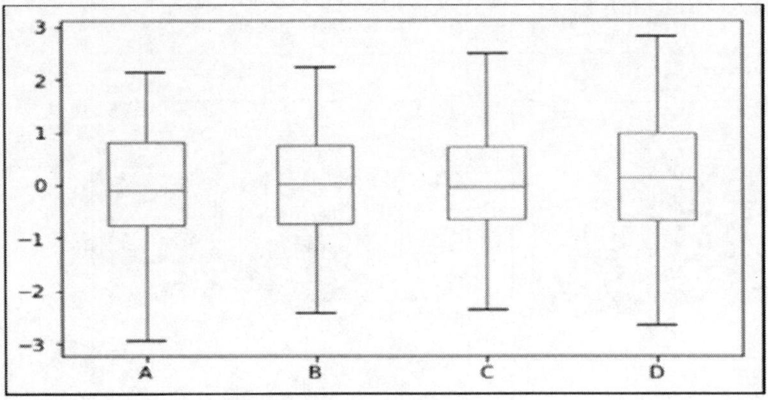

Fig. 14.7: Box plot

14.1.4 Area Plot

Area plot can be created using the **Series.plot.area()** or the **DataFrame.plot.area()** methods.

Example

```
import pandas as pd
import numpy as np
df = pd.DataFrame(np.random.rand(10, 4), columns=['a', 'b', 'c', 'd'])
df.plot.area()
```

Its **output** is as follows

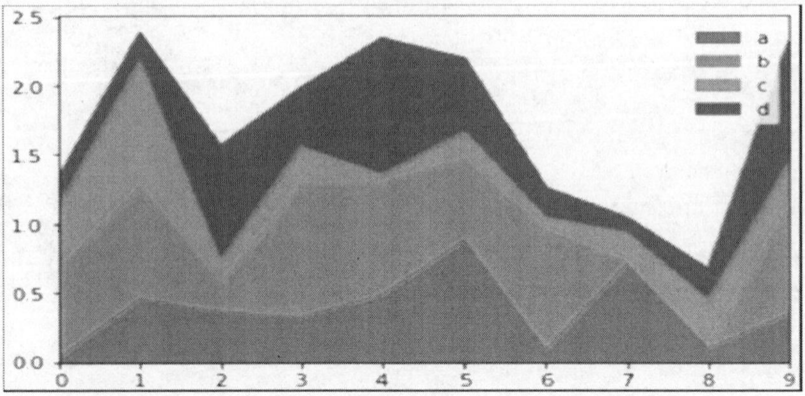

Fig. 14.8: Area plot

14.1.5 Scatter Plot

Scatter plot can be created using the **DataFrame.plot.scatter()** methods.

Example

```
import pandas as pd
import numpy as np
df = pd.DataFrame(np.random.rand(50, 4), columns=['a', 'b', 'c', 'd'])
df.plot.scatter(x='a', y='b')
```

Its **output** is as follows:

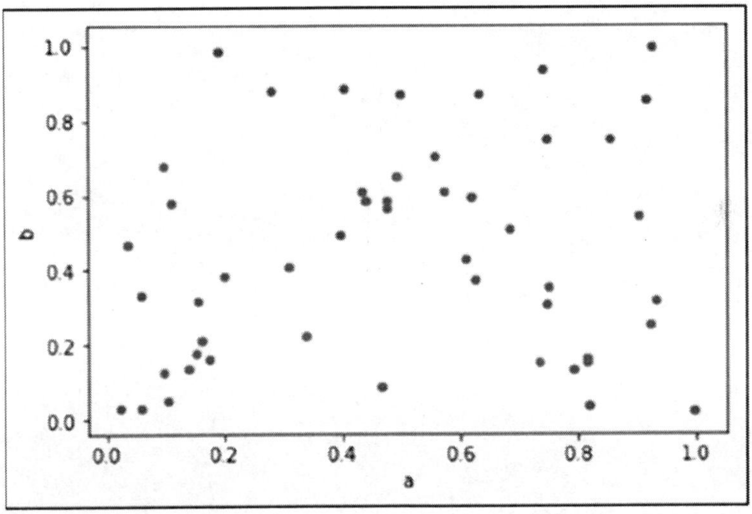

Fig. 14.9: Scatter plot

14.1.6 Pie Chart

Pie chart can be created using the **DataFrame.plot.pie()** method.

Example

```
import pandas as pd
import numpy as np
df = pd.DataFrame(3 * np.random.rand(4), index=['a', 'b', 'c', 'd'],
columns=['x'])
df.plot.pie(subplots=True)
```

Its **output** is as follows:

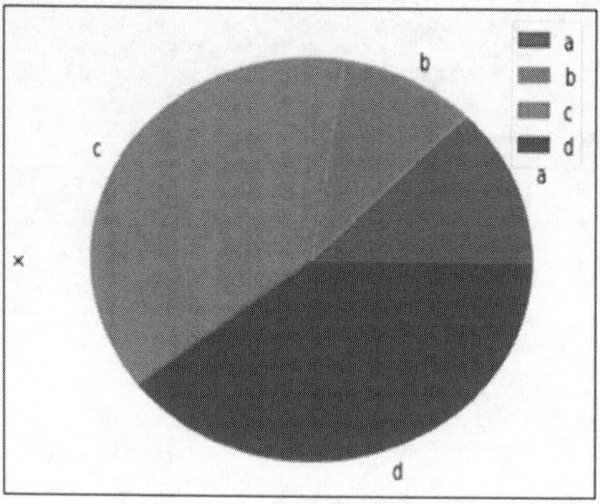

Fig. 14.10: Pie plot

15

Data Visualization

15.1 Data Visualization

Data visualization is the graphical representation of information and data. By using different visual elements like charts, graphs and maps. Data visualization tool provides easy way to see the understand the data and related trend/pattern.

1. There are multiple tools available for data visualization using which we can perform data visualization.
2. In python we can use a library called "matplot" for data visualization.
3. Python based plotting library "matplotlib" enables us to produce 2D as well as 3D graphics i.e. charts/graphs.
4. Pyplot interface of matplotlib is used for representing 2D graphs.

15.2 How to Install Matplotlib

1. Open "command promt" with administrator rights.
2. Here type "python –m pip install matplotlib" and press enter key.
3. In case this command is showing an error it means that you have not set python to "path" variable. You need to set the path (For this different set of instruction are there)
4. Note that internet connection is required for installation of matplotlib library.

15.3 Pyplot

1. Pyplot is a collection of command type functions that is used for data visualization. Its is available inside matplotlib library.
2. Pyplot interface provides many method for 2D plotting of data using which we can draw different types of 2D graphs/charts. We can draw different types of graphs/charts using pyplot methods i.e. plot(), bar() etc.

3. Multiple types of charts graphs can be plotted using pyplot like chart, bar chart, pie chart, scattered chart, histogram etc.
4. To use pyplot we can have to import matplotlib which can be done by two types

(i) Import matplotlib

(ii) Import matplotlib.pyplot as plt

15.4 Line chart

A line chart or line graph is a type of chart which displays information as a series of data points called 'markers' connected by straight line segments.

Example

```
import matplotlib.pyplot
x=[2,4,6,8,10]
y=[5,2,6,4,8]
matplotlib.pyplot.plot(x,y)
matplotlib.pyplot.show()
```

15.4.1 Customization of Plots

Here, we discuss some elementary customizations applicable to almost any plot.

parameters

color: This is used to set color of the line, This color could be any valid color.

Markeredgecolor: This is used to set color of marker. This color could be any valid color.

Character	Color
b	blue
g	green
r	red
m	magenta
y	yellow
k	black
c	cyan
w	white

line style attributes
#'solid','dashed','dashdot','dotted'

Example

```
import matplotlib.pyplot as plt
x=[5,10,15,20,25]
y=[10,14,7,15,16]
plt.plot(x,y, color='r',marker='*',
markeredgecolor='b',markersize=8,linewidth=10,linestyle="dotted")
plt.show()
```

Output:

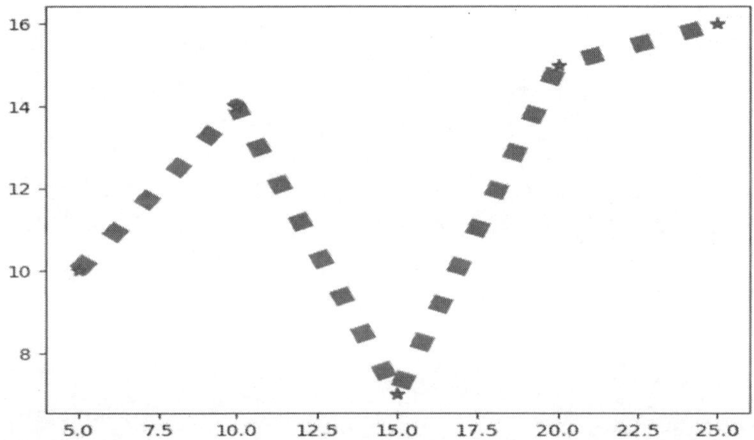

Example

```
import matplotlib.pyplot as plt
# x axis values
x = [1,2,3,4,5,6]
# corresponding y axis values
y = [2,4,1,5,2,6]
# plotting the points
plt.plot(x, y, color='green', linestyle='dashed', linewidth = 3,
      marker=›o›, markerfacecolor=›blue›, markersize=12)
# setting x and y axis range
plt.ylim(1,8)
plt.xlim(1,8)
# naming the x axis
plt.xlabel('x - axis')
# naming the y axis
plt.ylabel('y - axis')
```

```
# giving a title to my graph
plt.title('Some cool customizations!')
# function to show the plot
plt.show()
```

Output

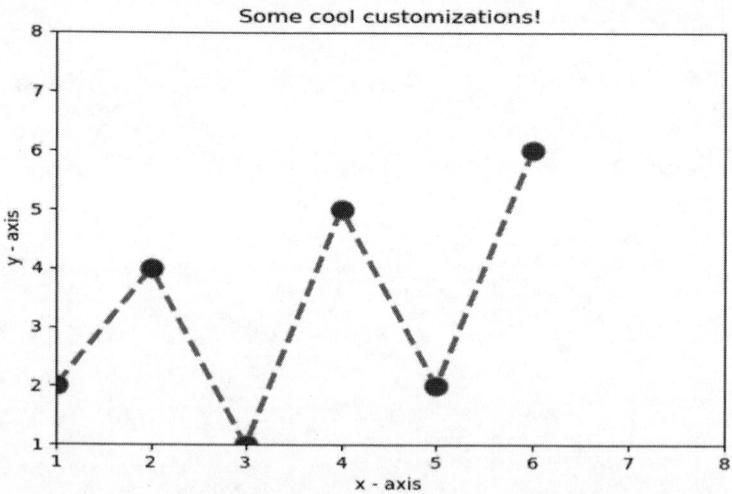

Note:

As you can see, we have done several customizations like:

- setting the line-width, line-style, line-color.
- setting the marker, marker's face color, marker's size.
- overriding the x and y-axis range. If overriding is not done, pyplot module uses the auto-scale feature to set the axis range and scale.

15.5 Multiple plots on the same axis

Here we will see how to add 2 plots within the same axis.

Example

```
import matplotlib.pyplot as plt
import numpy as np
x = np.array([1, 2, 3, 4])
y = x*2
# first plot with X and Y data
plt.plot(x, y)
```

```
x1 = [2, 4, 6, 8]
y1 = [3, 5, 7, 9]
# second plot with x1 and y1 data
plt.plot(x1, y1, '-.')
plt.xlabel("X-axis data")
plt.ylabel("Y-axis data")
plt.title('multiple plots')
plt.show()
```

Output

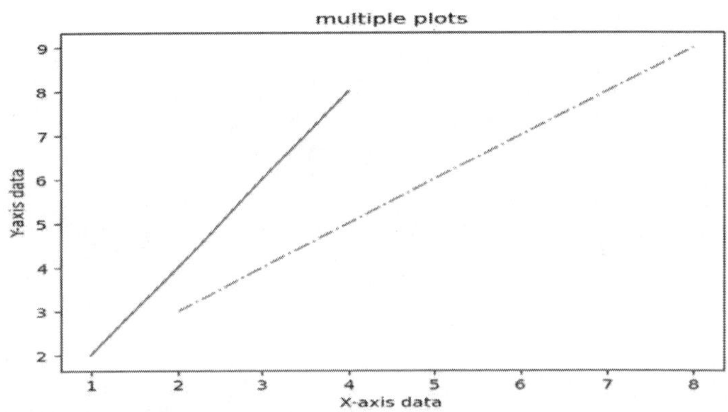

Example

```
import matplotlib.pyplot as plt
# line 1 points
x1 = [1,2,3]
y1 = [2,4,1]
# plotting the line 1 points
plt.plot(x1, y1, label = "line 1")
# line 2 points
x2 = [1,2,3]
y2 = [4,1,3]
# plotting the line 2 points
plt.plot(x2, y2, label = "line 2")
# naming the x axis
plt.xlabel('x - axis')
# naming the y axis
plt.ylabel('y - axis')
# giving a title to my graph
```

```
plt.title('Two lines on same graph!')
# show a legend on the plot
plt.legend()
# function to show the plot
plt.show()
```

Output

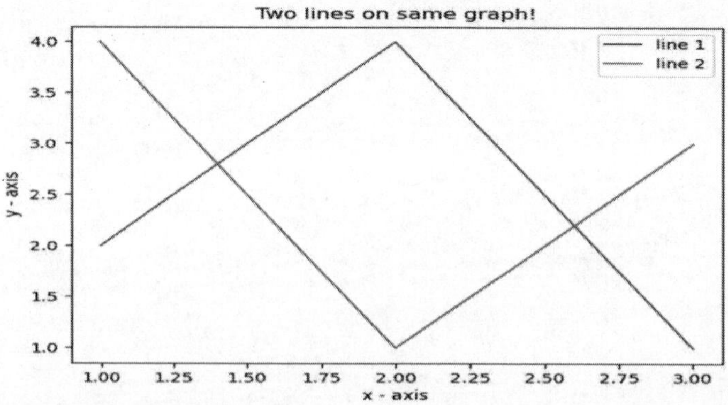

- Note: Here, we plot two lines on the same graph. We differentiate between them by giving them a name(**label**) which is passed as an argument of the .plot() function.
- The small rectangular box giving information about the type of line and its color is called a legend. We can add a legend to our plot using **.legend()** function.

15.6 Fill the Area Between Two Plots

Using the **pyplot.fill_between()** function we can fill in the region between two line plots in the same graph. This will help us in understanding the margin of data between two line plots based on certain conditions.

Example

```
import matplotlib.pyplot as plt
import numpy as np
x = np.array([1, 2, 3, 4])
y = x*2
plt.plot(x, y)
x1 = [2, 4, 6, 8]
y1 = [3, 5, 7, 9]
```

```
plt.plot(x, y1, '-.')
plt.xlabel("X-axis data")
plt.ylabel("Y-axis data")
plt.title('multiple plots')
plt.fill_between(x, y, y1, color='green', alpha=0.5)
plt.show()
```

Output

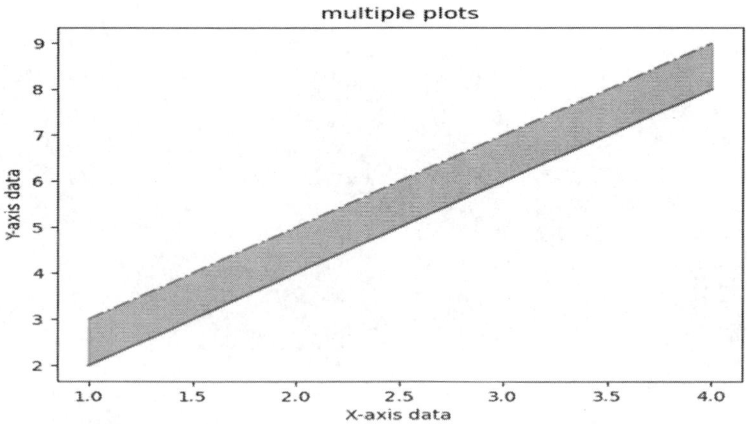

15.7 Bar Chart

A bar chart or Bar graph is a type of chart which displays information as a series of line of rectangle with a height and length.

Example

```
import matplotlib.pyplot as plt
# x-coordinates of left sides of bars
left = [1, 2, 3, 4, 5]
# heights of bars
height = [10, 24, 36, 40, 5]
# labels for bars
tick_label = ['one', 'two', 'three', 'four', 'five']
# plotting a bar chart
plt.bar(left, height, tick_label = tick_label,
    width = 0.8, color = [‹red›, ‹green›])
# naming the x-axis
plt.xlabel('x - axis')
# naming the y-axis
plt.ylabel('y - axis')
```

```
# plot title
plt.title('My bar chart!')
# function to show the plot

plt.show()
```

Output

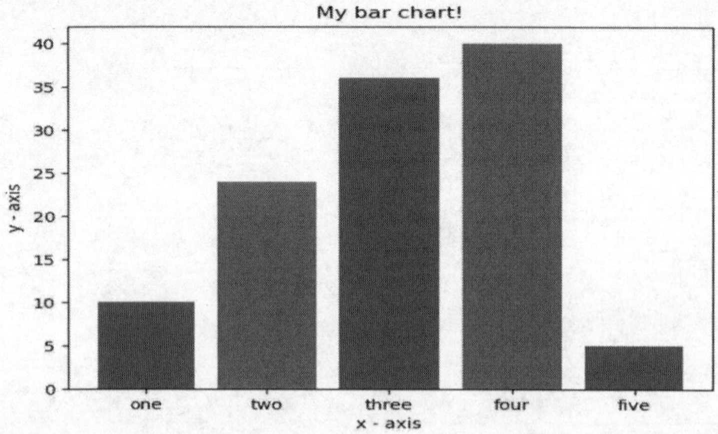

Note

- Here, we use **plt.bar()** function to plot a bar chart.
- x-coordinates of the left side of bars are passed along with the heights of bars.
- you can also give some names to x-axis coordinates by defining **tick_ labels**

15.8 Pie chart

A pie chart or pie graph is a type of chart which a circle is divided into sectors that each represents a proportion of the whole.

Example

```
import matplotlib.pyplot as plt
# defining labels
activities = ['eat', 'sleep', 'work', 'play']
# portion covered by each label
slices = [3, 7, 8, 6]
# color for each label
```

```
colors = ['r', 'y', 'g', 'b']
# plotting the pie chart
plt.pie(slices, labels = activities, colors=colors,
    startangle=90, shadow = True, explode = (0, 0, 0.1, 0),
    radius = 1.2, autopct = ‹%1.1f%%›)
# plotting legend
plt.legend()
# showing the plot
plt.show()
```

Output

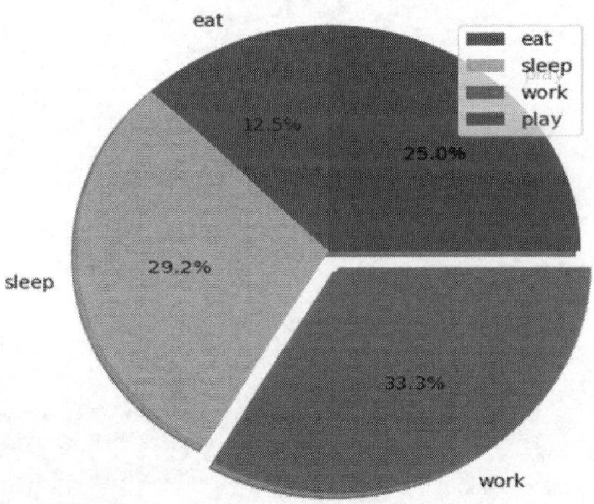

Note:

- Here, we plot a pie chart by using **plt.pie()** method.
- First of all, we define the **labels** using a list called **activities**.
- Then, a portion of each label can be defined using another list called **slices**.
- Color for each label is defined using a list called **colors**.
- **shadow = True** will show a shadow beneath each label in pie chart.
- **startangle** rotates the start of the pie chart by given degrees counterclockwise from the x-axis.
- **explode** is used to set the fraction of radius with which we offset each wedge.

- **autopct** is used to format the value of each label. Here, we have set it to show the percentage value only upto 1 decimal place.

15.9 Histogram

A histogram is graphical display of data using bars of different heights. In a histogram, each bar groups numbers into ranges. Taller bar shows that more data falls into that range.

Example

```
import matplotlib.pyplot as plt
# frequencies
ages = [2,5,70,40,30,45,50,45,43,40,44,
      60,7,13,57,18,90,77,32,21,20,40]
# setting the ranges and no. of intervals
range = (0, 100)
bins = 10
# plotting a histogram
plt.hist(ages, bins, range, color = ‘green’,
      histtype = ‘bar’, rwidth = 0.8)
# x-axis label
plt.xlabel(‘age’)
# frequency label
plt.ylabel(‘No. of people’)
# plot title
plt.title(‘My histogram’)
# function to show the plot
plt.show()
```

Output

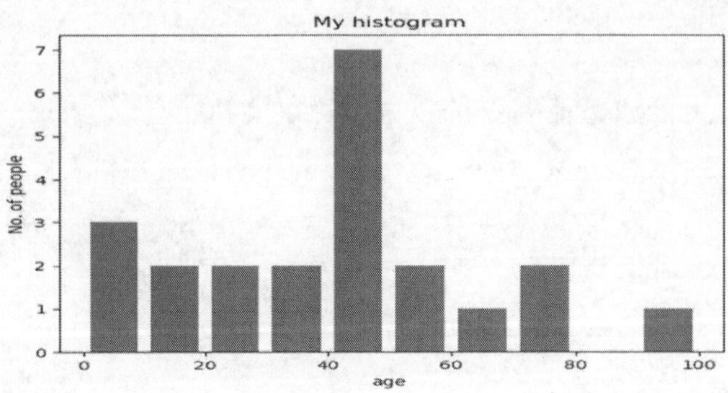

Note

- Here, we use **plt.hist()** function to plot a histogram.
- frequencies are passed as the **ages** list.
- The range could be set by defining a tuple containing min and max values.
- The next step is to "**bin**" the range of values—that is, divide the entire range of values into a series of intervals—and then count how many values fall into each interval. Here we have defined **bins** = 10. So, there are a total of 100/10 = 10 intervals

15.10 Scatter Plot

- Here, we use **plt.scatter()** function to plot a scatter plot.
- As a line, we define x and corresponding y-axis values here as well.
- **marker** argument is used to set the character to use as a marker. Its size can be defined using the **s** parameter.

Example

```
import matplotlib.pyplot as plt
# x-axis values
x = [1,2,3,4,5,6,7,8,9,10]
# y-axis values
y = [2,4,5,7,6,8,9,11,12,12]
# plotting points as a scatter plot
plt.scatter(x, y, label= "stars", color= "green",
        marker= «*», s=30)
# x-axis label
plt.xlabel('x - axis')
# frequency label
plt.ylabel('y - axis')
# plot title
plt.title('My scatter plot!')
# showing legend
plt.legend()
# function to show the plot
plt.show()
```

Output

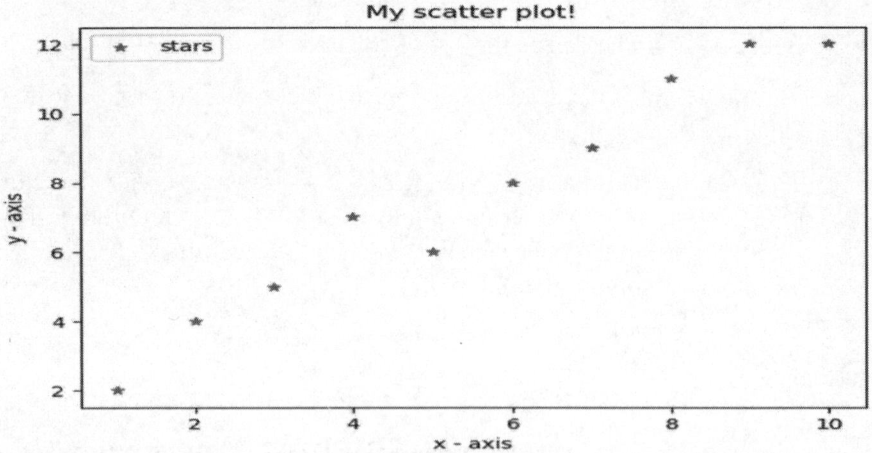

15.11 Plotting Curves of Given Equation

Here, we use **NumPy** which is a general-purpose array-processing package in python.

- To set the x-axis values, we use the **np.arange()** method in which the first two arguments are for range and the third one for step-wise increment. The result is a NumPy array.
- To get corresponding y-axis values, we simply use the predefined **np.sin()** method on the NumPy array.
- Finally, we plot the points by passing x and y arrays to the **plt.plot()** function.

Example

```
# importing the required modules
import matplotlib.pyplot as plt
import numpy as np
# setting the x - coordinates
x = np.arange(0, 2*(np.pi), 0.1)
# setting the corresponding y - coordinates
y = np.sin(x)
# plotting the points
plt.plot(x, y)
# function to show the plot
plt.show()
```

15.12 Subplot

Subplots are required when we want to show two or more plots in same figure. We can do it in two ways using two slightly different methods.

Method 1

```
# importing required modules
import matplotlib.pyplot as plt
import numpy as np
# function to generate coordinates
def create_plot(ptype):
    # setting the x-axis values
    x = np.arange(-10, 10, 0.01)
    # setting the y-axis values
    if ptype == 'linear':
        y = x
    elif ptype == 'quadratic':
        y = x**2
    elif ptype == 'cubic':
        y = x**3
    elif ptype == 'quartic':
        y = x**4
    return(x, y)
# setting a style to use
plt.style.use('fivethirtyeight')
# create a figure
fig = plt.figure()
# define subplots and their positions in figure
plt1 = fig.add_subplot(221)
plt2 = fig.add_subplot(222)
plt3 = fig.add_subplot(223)
plt4 = fig.add_subplot(224)
# plotting points on each subplot
x, y = create_plot('linear')
plt1.plot(x, y, color ='r')
plt1.set_title('$y_1 = x$')
x, y = create_plot('quadratic')
plt2.plot(x, y, color ='b')
plt2.set_title('$y_2 = x^2$')
x, y = create_plot('cubic')
plt3.plot(x, y, color ='g')
```

```
plt3.set_title('$y_3 = x^3$')
x, y = create_plot('quartic')
plt4.plot(x, y, color ='k')
plt4.set_title('$y_4 = x^4$')
# adjusting space between subplots
fig.subplots_adjust(hspace=.5,wspace=0.5)
# function to show the plot
plt.show()
```

output

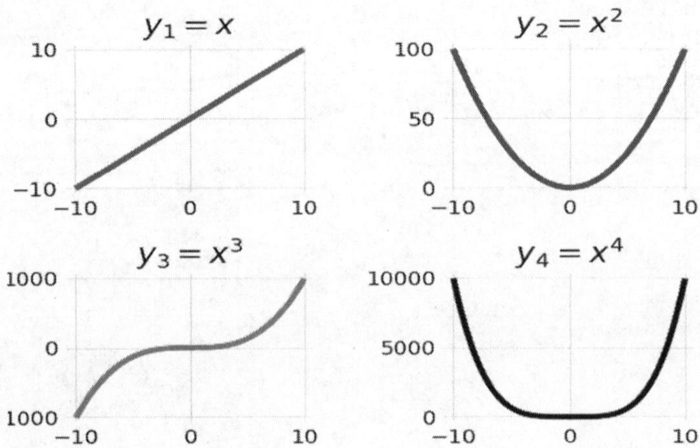

Method 2

```
# importing required modules
import matplotlib.pyplot as plt
import numpy as np
# function to generate coordinates
def create_plot(ptype):
    # setting the x-axis values
    x = np.arange(0, 5, 0.01)
    # setting y-axis values
    if ptype == 'sin':
        # a sine wave
        y = np.sin(2*np.pi*x)
    elif ptype == 'exp':
        # negative exponential function
        y = np.exp(-x)
    elif ptype == 'hybrid':
```

```
        # a damped sine wave
        y = (np.sin(2*np.pi*x))*(np.exp(-x))
    return(x, y)
# setting a style to use
plt.style.use('ggplot')
# defining subplots and their positions
plt1 = plt.subplot2grid((11,1), (0,0), rowspan = 3, colspan = 1)
plt2 = plt.subplot2grid((11,1), (4,0), rowspan = 3, colspan = 1)
plt3 = plt.subplot2grid((11,1), (8,0), rowspan = 3, colspan = 1)
# plotting points on each subplot
x, y = create_plot('sin')
plt1.plot(x, y, label = 'sine wave', color ='b')
x, y = create_plot('exp')
plt2.plot(x, y, label = 'negative exponential', color = 'r')
x, y = create_plot('hybrid')
plt3.plot(x, y, label = 'damped sine wave', color = 'g')
# show legends of each subplot
plt1.legend()
plt2.legend()
plt3.legend()
# function to show plot
plt.show()
```

Output

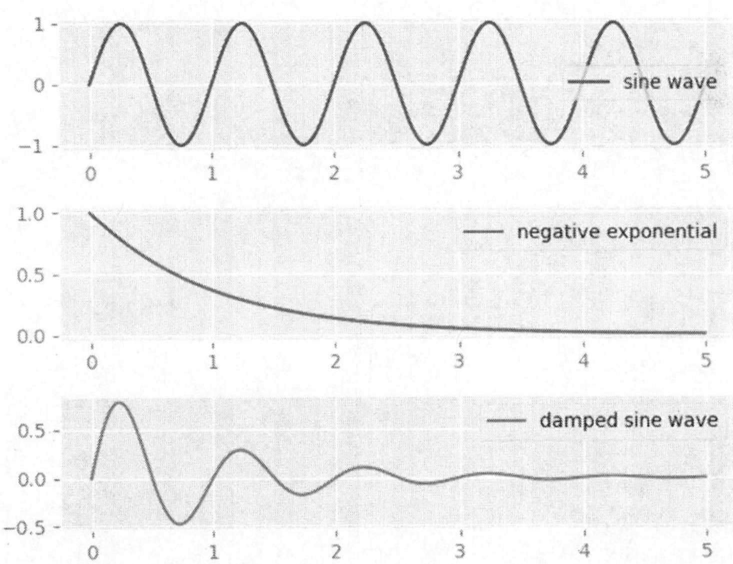

15.13 3-D Plotting

We can easily plot 3-D figures in matplotlib. Now, we discuss some important and commonly used 3-D plots.

- Plotting points

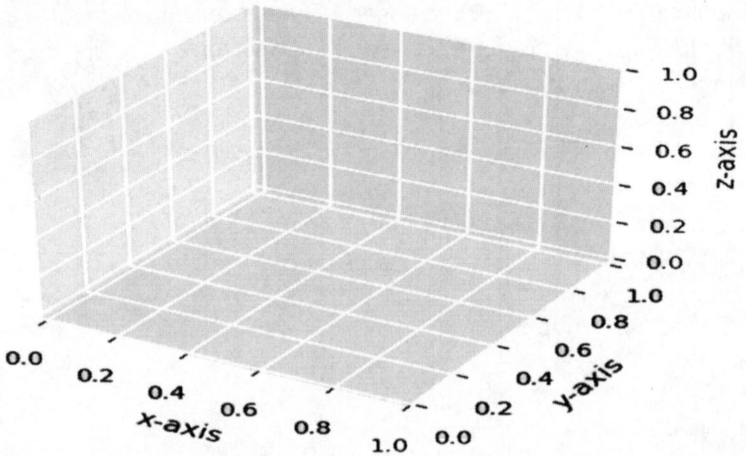

Note

- Let us try to understand some important aspects of this code now.

  from mpl_toolkits.mplot3d import axes3d

- This is the module required to plot on 3-D space.

  ax1 = fig.add_subplot(111, projection='3d')

- Here, we create a subplot on our figure and set projection argument as 3d.

  ax1.scatter(x, y, z, c = 'm', marker = 'o')

- Now we use **.scatter()** function to plot the points in XYZ plane.
- Plotting lines

Example

```
# importing required modules
from mpl_toolkits.mplot3d import axes3d
import matplotlib.pyplot as plt
from matplotlib import style
```

```
import numpy as np
# setting a custom style to use
style.use('ggplot')
# create a new figure for plotting
fig = plt.figure()
# create a new subplot on our figure
ax1 = fig.add_subplot(111, projection='3d')
# defining x, y, z co-ordinates
x = np.random.randint(0, 10, size = 5)
y = np.random.randint(0, 10, size = 5)
z = np.random.randint(0, 10, size = 5)
# plotting the points on subplot
ax1.plot_wireframe(x,y,z)
# setting the labels
ax1.set_xlabel('x-axis')
ax1.set_ylabel('y-axis')
ax1.set_zlabel('z-axis')
plt.show()
```

Output

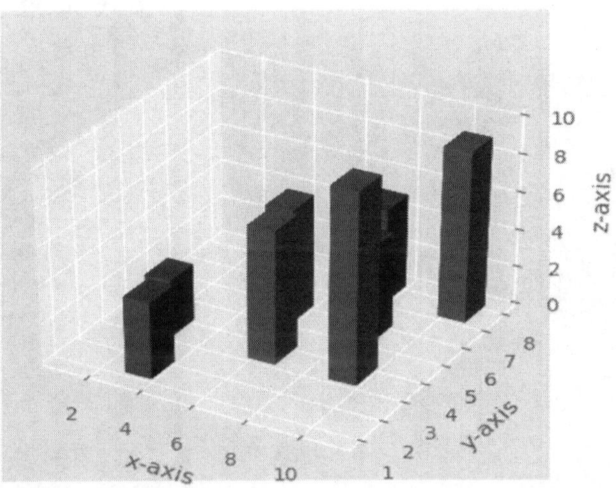

Note

- Let us go through important aspects of this program:

  x = [1,2,3,4,5,6,7,8,9,10]

  y = [4,3,1,6,5,3,7,5,3,7]

```
z = np.zeros(10)
```

- Here, we define the base positions of bars. Setting z = 0 means all bars start from XY plane.

```
dx = np.ones(10)             # length along x-axis
dy = np.ones(10)             # length along y-axs
dz = [1,3,4,2,6,7,5,5,10,9]  # height of bar
```

- dx, dy, dz denote the size of bar. Consider he bar as a cuboid, then dx, dy, dz are its expansions along x, y, z axis respectively.

```
for h in dz:
 if h > 5:
   color.append('r')
else:
 color.append('b')
```

- Here, we set the color for each bar as a list. The color scheme is red for bars with height greater than 5 and blue otherwise.

```
ax1.bar3d(x, y, z, dx, dy, dz, color = color)
```

- Finally, to plot the bars, we use **.bar3d()** function.
- Plotting curves

Example

```
# importing required modules
from mpl_toolkits.mplot3d import axes3d
import matplotlib.pyplot as plt
from matplotlib import style
import numpy as np
# setting a custom style to use
style.use('ggplot')
# create a new figure for plotting
fig = plt.figure()
# create a new subplot on our figure
ax1 = fig.add_subplot(111, projection='3d')
# get points for a mesh grid
u, v = np.mgrid[0:2*np.pi:200j, 0:np.pi:100j]
# setting x, y, z co-ordinates
```

```
x=np.cos(u)*np.sin(v)
y=np.sin(u)*np.sin(v)
z=np.cos(v)
# plotting the curve
ax1.plot_wireframe(x, y, z, rstride = 5, cstride = 5, linewidth = 1)
plt.show()
```

Output

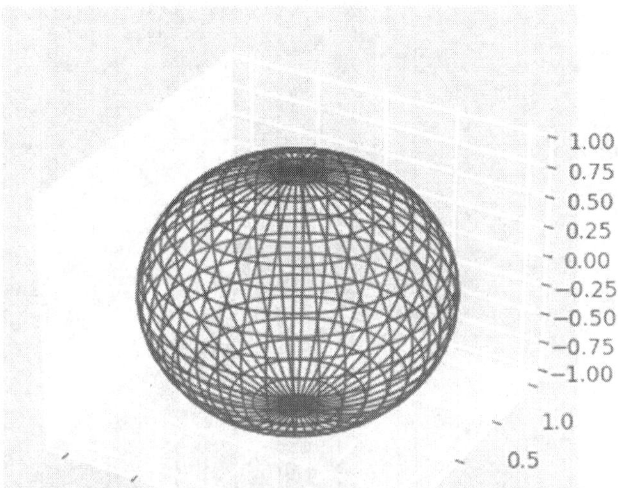

Note

- Here, we plotted a sphere as a mesh grid. Let us go through some important parts:

  u, v = np.mgrid[0:2*np.pi:200j, 0:np.pi:100j]

- We use np.mgrid in order to get points so that we can create a mesh. You can read more about this here.

  x=np.cos(u)*np.sin(v)

  y=np.sin(u)*np.sin(v)

  z=np.cos(v)

- This is nothing but the parametric equation of a sphere.

  ax1.plot_wireframe(x, y, z, rstride = 5, cstride = 5, linewidth = 1)

- Agan, we use **.plot_wireframe()** method. Here, **rstride** and **cstride** arguments can be used to set how much dense our mesh must be.

15.14 Matplotlib Graph Plotting Using Object Oriented API

Example

```
# importing matplotlib library
import matplotlib.pyplot as plt
# x axis values
x =[0, 5, 3, 6, 8, 4, 5, 7]
# y axis values
y =[5, 3, 6, 3, 7, 5, 6, 8]
# creating the canvas
fig = plt.figure()
# setting the size of canvas
axes = fig.add_axes([0, 0, 1, 1])
# plotting the graph
axes.plot(x, y, 'mo--')

# displaying the graph
plt.show()
```

Output:

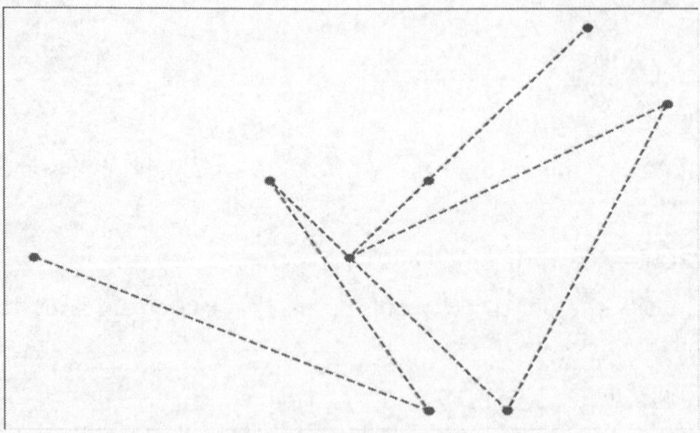

Note

Everything is pretty much clear in the first example but there is a thing that needs to be focused on, "Setting size of the canvas", what this basically means is to set the size of the figure on which you want to plot the graph, the syntax is like this.

```
add_axes([left, bottom, width, height])
```

The values of left, bottom, height and width lies between 0 to 1. Another example will make you more clear about this concept.

Example

```
# importing matplotlib library
import matplotlib.pyplot as plt
# x-axis values
x =[0, 1, 2, 3, 4, 5, 6]
# y-axis values
y =[0, 1, 3, 6, 9, 12, 17]
# creating the canvas
fig = plt.figure()
# setting size of first canvas
axes1 = fig.add_axes([0, 0, 0.7, 1])
# plotting graph of first canvas
axes1.plot(x, y, 'mo--')
# setting size of second canvas
axes2 = fig.add_axes([0.1, 0.5, 0.3, 0.3])
# plotting graph of second canvas
axes2.plot(x, y, 'go--')
# displaying both graphs
plt.show()
```

Output

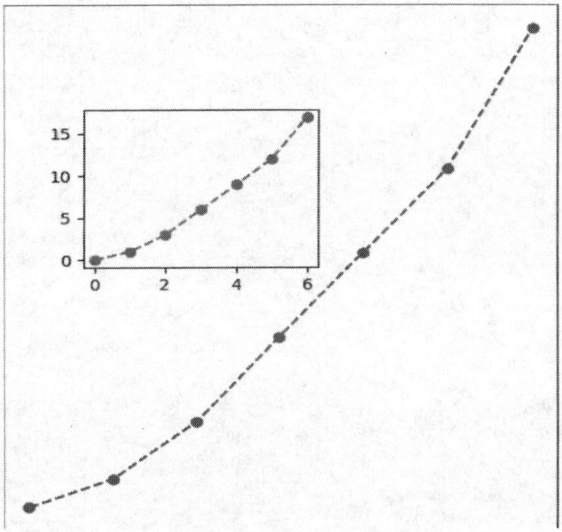

16

Object Oriented Programming in Python

16.1 OOP in python

Object-oriented programming (OOP) is a programming language model which organized object and data.

16.1.1 What is Encapsulation

If same variable is reapet in two different palce then which problem is solved using encapsulation it means one variable is making private otherwise program generate error.

16.1.2 Abstraction

Abstraction in Python is the process of hiding the real implementation of an application from the user and emphasizing only on usage of it. For example, consider you have bought a new electronic gadget. Along with the gadget, you get a user guide, instructing how to use the application, but this user guide has no info regarding the internal working of the gadget.

Another example is, when you use TV remote, you do not know how pressing a key in the remote changes the channel internally on the TV. You just know that pressing + volume key will increase the volume.

16.1.3 Why Do We Need Abstraction?

Through the process of abstraction in Python, a programmer can hide all the irrelevant data/process of an application in order to reduce complexity and increase efficiency.

16.1.4 Inheritance in Python

Inheritance is the capability of one class to derive or inherit the properties from another class. The benefits of inheritance are:

1. It represents real-world relationships well.
2. It provides **reusability** of a code. We don't have to write the same code again and again. Also, it allows us to add more features to a class without modifying it.
3. It is transitive in nature, which means that if class B inherits from another class A, then all the subclasses of B would automatically inherit from class A.

16.1.5 Polymorphism in Python

- It means we can use same method/function name for different types.
- If a variable, object or method perform different behaviour according to situation, it is called polymorphism.

16.2 Class in OOP

Class:A python class is a group of attributes and methods.

What is attribute: attributes are represented by variable the contain data

What is method: Method performs an action or task. It is similar to function.

Method three type

(i) Instance method (ii) class method (iii) static method

16.2.1 How to Create to Class

Syntax1:

```
Class classname(object):
  def __init__(self):  #constructor
    self.variable_name=value  #attributes
   self.variable_name='value'
  def method_name(self):
     Body of method
```

OR

```
Class classname(object):
  def __init__(self):  #constructor
    self.variable_name=value  #attributes
   self.variable_name='value'
  def method_name(self):
     Body of method
```

Syntax2:

```
Class classname(object):
   def __init__(self):  #constructor
      self.variable_name=value   #attributes
     self.variable_name='value'
   def method_name(self):
       Body of method
      def method_name(self, f1, f2):  #f1, f2 are formal argument
       Body of method
```

OR

```
Class classname:
   def __init__(self, f1, f2):  #constructor #f1, f2 are formal argument
      self.variable_name=value   #attributes
     self.variable_name='value'
   def method_name(self):
       Body of method
      def method_name(self, f1, f2):  #f1, f2 are formal argument
       Body of method
```

Class: class keyword is used to create a class

Object: object represents the base class name from where all classes in python are derived. This class is also derived from object class. This is optional

__init__(): This method is use to initialize the variable. This is a special method. We do not call this method explicitly.

Self: self is a variable which refers to current class instance/object

Example

```
class computer:
   def feature(self):  #self as pointer it is take object atumatically
      print("i5,8gb,1tb")
com1=computer()    #object it means taken raw material for making
computer
com2=computer()
computer.feature(com1) #1st method for parameter pass this is given for
final shape for computer
com2.feature()  #2nd method for parameter pass
```

Object: object is class type variable or class instance. To use a class we should create an object to class

Syntax:

```
Object_name=class_name()
Object_name=class_name(arg)
```

Example without argument

```
Class Mobile:
 def_init_(self):
   self.model='RealMe X'
 def show_model(self):
   print('model:', self.model)
realme=Mobile()  #object call
```

Note:

```
realme=Mobile()

realme.model # method call
```

- A block of memory is allocated on heap. The size of allocated memory be decided from the attributes and method available in the class (Mobile).
- After allocating memory, the special method_init_() is called internally. This method stores the initial data into the variables.
- The allocated memory location adrdress of the instance is returned into object(realMe)
- The memory location is passed to self

16.2.2 Accessing Class Member Using Object

We can access variable and method of a class using object or instance of class.

Syntax:

```
Object_name.method_name  #method call

Object_name.method_name(parameter list)
```

Self: self is a default variable that contains the memory address of the current object

This variable is used to refer all the instance variable and method.

Example with argument

```
Class Mobile:
 def_init_(self, m):
   self.model=m
```

```
  def show_model(self):
    print('model:', self.model)
realme=Mobile('RealMe X')   #object call
```

16.2.3 Constructor in Python

- Python supports a special type of method called constructor for initializing the instance variable of a class.
- A constructor is called only once at the time of creating an instance.
- If two instances are created for a class, theconstructor will be called once for each instance.

ExampleConstructor without parameter

```
Class Mobile:
  def_init_(self):
    self.model='RealMe X'
realme=Mobile()  #object call
```

ExampleConstructor with parameter

```
Class Mobile:
  def_init_(self, m):
    self.model=m

realme=Mobile('RealMe X')   #object call
```

Type of variable

(i) Instance variable (ii) class variable or static variable

Example Instance variable

```
class computer:
   def __init__(self,ram,hd): #for define instance variable or value define
within function
      self.ram=ram
      self.hd=hd
   def feature(self):   #self as pointer it is take object atumatically and this
method instance method
      print("your computer config is:",self.ram,self.hd)
com1=computer("8gb","1tb")    #object it means taken raw material for
making computer
com2=computer("16gb", "2tb")
```

computer.feature(com1) #1st method for parameter pass this is given for final shape for computer
com2.feature() #2nd method for parameter pass

16.2.4 Accessing Instance Variable

With instance method to access instance variable, we need instance methods with self as first parameter then we can access instance variable using self. variable_name

Example

```
Class Mobile:
  def_init_(self):
    self.model='RealMe X'   #instance variable
  def show_model(self):  #instance method
     self.model  #accessing instance variable
realme=Mobile()  #object call
```

outside class

we can access instance variable using object_name.variable_name

```
Class Mobile:
  def_init_(self):
    self.model='RealMe X'   #instance variable
  def show_model(self):  #instance method
     print(self.model)  #accessing instance variable within the class
realme=Mobile()  #object call
realme.model  #accessing instance variable outside class
```

Example

```
class computer:
   def __init__(self,ram,hd,pro):
      self.ram=ram
      self.hd=hd
      self.pro="i5"
   def feature(self):  #self as pointer it is take object atumatically and this
method instance method
      print("your computer config is:",self.ram,self.hd,self.pro)
com1=computer("8gb","1tb",pro="i6")    #object it means taken raw
material for making computer
com2=computer("16gb", "2tb",pro="i5")
com1.pro="i6"
```

computer.feature(com1) #1st method for parameter pass this is given for final shape for computer
com2.feature() #2nd method for parameter pass
Note: init function automatically call

Note which method use only instance variable it is called instance method. This type method not use class variable or static variable

16.2.5 Class Variable/static Variable

Class variables are the variables whose single copy is available to all the instance of the class. If we modify the copy of the class variable in instance, it will effect all the copies in the other instance.

Example

```
Class mobile:
   fp='yes'    #class variable
   def_init_(self):
      self.model='realme x'
  def show_model(self):
        print(self.model)
realme=mobile()
```

16.2.6 Accessing Class/ Static Variable

With class method

To access class variable, we need class methods with cls as first parameter then we can access class variable using cls.variable_name

Example

```
Class mobile:
   fp='yes'    #class variable
   def_init_(self):
      self.model='realme x'
  def show_model(self):
        print(self.model)
@classmethod    #class method
def is_fp(cls):
   cls.fp    #accessing class variable inside class method
realme=mobile()
```

With class method

We can access class variable using Classname.variable_name

Example

```
Class mobile:
   fp='yes'    #class variable
   def_init_(self):
      self.model='realme x'
  def show_model(self):
      print(self.model)
@classmethod   #class method
def is_fp(cls):
   cls.fp    #accessing class variable inside class method
realme=mobile()
mobile.fp    #accessing class variable outside class
```

Note: Class variables are the variables whose single copy is available to all the instance of the class. If we modify the copy of the class variable in instance, it will effect all the copies in the other instance.

Example

```
class mobile:
      fp='yes'
   def_init_(self):
      self.model='realme x'
  def show_model(self):
      print(self.model)
   @classmethod
    def show_model(cls):
        print("Fingerprint:",cls.fp) #accessing class variable inside class
method
realme=mobile()
realme.show_model()
mobile.is_fp
print()
mobile.fp='No'  #change class value out side method
mobile.is_fp
```

Example Multiple object

```
class mobile:
      fp='yes'
```

```
  @classmethod
   def show_model(cls):
       print("Fingerprint:",cls.fp) #accessing class variable inside class
method
realme=mobile()
redmi=mobile()
geek=mobile()
print("RealMe:", mobile.fp)
print("Remi:", mobile.fp)
print("geek:", mobile.fp)
print()
mobile.fp='No'  #change class value out side method
print("RealMe:", mobile.fp)
print("Remi:", mobile.fp)
print("geek:", mobile.fp)
```

Class Method

class method are the methods which act upon the class variable or ststic variable of the class.

decorator @classmethod need to write above the class method

By default, the first parameter of class method is cls which refers to the class itself.

Syntax:

```
@classmethod
def method_name(cls):  # class method without parameter
      method body
```

Example

```
class mobile:
      fp='yes'
  @classmethod
   def show_model(cls):
       print("Fingerprint:",cls.fp)
realme=mobile()
mobile.show_model()  #calling class method without argument
```

calling class method

syntax: classname.method_name()

class method with parameter

```
@classmethod
def method_name(cls,f1,f2): # class method with parameter
      method body
```

Example

```
class mobile:
    fp='yes'
   @classmethod
    def show_model(cls,r):
        cls.ram=r
        print("Fingerprint:",cls.fp)
        print("RAM:",cls.ram)
realme=mobile()   #object
mobile.show_model('4GB')   #calling class method without argument
```

Calling class method

syntax: classname.method_name(actual_argument)

Accessing class/static variable

With class method: To access class variable, we need class methods with cls as first parameter then we can access class variable using cls.variable_name.

16.3 Namespace in Python Programming

In python, Namespace represents a memory block where names are mapped to objects.

Class Namespace-A class maintains it's own namespace known as class namespace. In the class namespace, the names are mapped to class variable.

Instance Namespace-Every instance have it's own name space know as instance namespace. In the instance namespace, the name are mapped to instance variable.

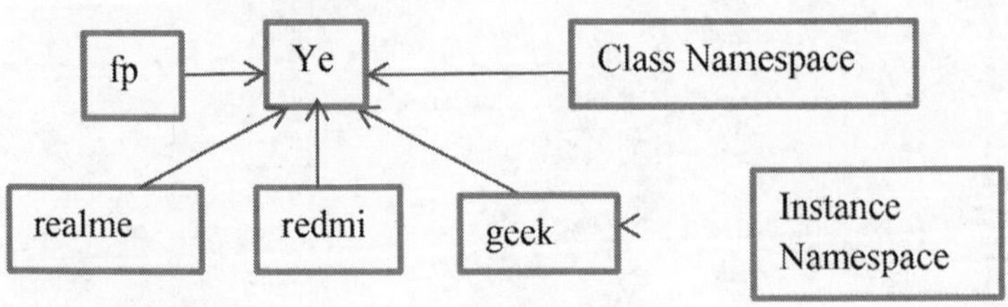


```
Class mobile:
   fp=yes  #class variable
realme=mobile()
redmi=mobile()
geek=mobile()
mobile.fp     #yes
```

realme.fp #yes
redmi.fp #yes
geek.fp #yes

Note: if change the any value using class name and class variable then effect instance object and class namespace both e.g

mobile.fp=no
mobile.fp #no
realme.fp #no
redmi.fp #no
geek.fp #no
but if change using the class variable and instance name then effect only single object e.g.
realme.fp=not working
mobile.fp #no
realme.fp # not working
redmi.fp #no
geek.fp #no

16.4 Type of Methods

16.4.1 Instance Methods

Instance method are the methods which act upon the instance variable of the class. Instance method need to know the memory address of the instance which is provided through *self* variable by defaults as first parameter for the instance method.

Syntax: without parameter

```
def method_name(self)
    Function body
```

Example

Syntax: with parameter

```
def method_name(self, f1, f2)
    Function body
```

calling instance method w/o argument

instance methods are bound to object of the class so we call instance method with object name.

syntax: object_name.method_name()

Class Mobile:

```
 def_init_(self):
   self.model='RealMe X'   #instance variable
 def show_model(self):   #instance method
     self.model   #accessing instance variable inside instance method
realme=Mobile()   #object call
realme.show_model()   # calling instance method w/o argument
```

synatax: calling instance method with argument

syntax: object_name.method_name(actual_argument)

Example

```
Class Mobile:
 def_init_(self):
   self.model='RealMe X'   #instance variable
 def show_model(self,p):   #instance method
      self.price=p  # instance variable
     print(self.model, self.price)
realme=Mobile()   #object call
realme.show_model(1000)   # calling instance method w/o argument
```

(i) Accessor methods (ii) mutator methods

16.4.2 Accessor Method

This method is used to access or rad data of the variables. This method do not modify the data in the variable. This is called as getter method.

Syntax: def get_value(self)

def get_result(self)

Example

```
Class Mobile:
 def_init_(self):
   self.model='RealMe X'   #instance variable
 def get_model(self):   #instance method
          return self.model
```

```
realme=Mobile()  #object call
m=realme.get_model()
```

16.4.3 Mutator Methods

This methods is used to access or read and modify data of the variable. This method modify the data in the variable. This is also called as setter method.

Syntax:

```
def set_value(self):
def set_result(self):
```

Example

```
Class Mobile:
  def_init_(self):
    self.model='RealMe X'   #instance variable
  def set_model(self):  #instance method
        self.model='RealMe 2'
realme=Mobile()  #object call
m=realme.set_model()
```

16.4.4 Class Method

- class method are the methods which act upon the class variable or ststic variable of the class.
- decorator @classmethod need to write above the class method
- By default, the first parameter of class method is cls which refers to the class itself.

  Syntax:

  ```
  @classmethod
  def method_name(cls):  # class method without parameter
        method body
  ```

Example

```
class mobile:
      fp='yes'
   @classmethod
    def show_model(cls):
        print("Fingerprint:",cls.fp)
realme=mobile()
mobile.show_model()  #calling class method without argument
```

Calling class method with argument

Example

```
class mobile:
      fp='yes'
   @classmethod
    def show_model(cls, r):
        cls.ram=r
        print(cls.fp, cls.ram)
realme=mobile()
mobile.show_model(101)   #calling class method with argument
```

Example Class variable or static variable and class method

```
class computer:
   name="dell" #class variable or static variable
   def __init__(self,ram,hd,pro):
      self.ram=ram
      self.hd=hd
      self.pro="i5"
   def feature(self):   #self as pointer it is take object atumatically
      print("your computer config is:",self.ram,self.hd,self.pro)
   @classmethod    #class method
   def company(cls):
      print("company name is:",cls.name)
com1=computer("8gb","1tb",pro="i6")    #object it means taken raw
material for making computer
com2=computer("16gb", "2tb",pro="i5")
com1.pro="i6"
computer.feature(com1) #1st method for parameter pass this is given for final
shape for computer
com2.feature()  #2nd method for parameter pass
com2.company()  #call classmethod
```

16.4.5 Static methods

Static methods are used when some processing is related to the class but not need the class or its instance to perform any work

When use static method when we want to pass some values from outside and perform some action in the method.

Decorator @staticmethod need to write above the static method

Syntax:

```
@staticmethod
def method_name():
    Mehod body
```

Or

```
@staticmethod
def method_name(f, f2):  #with parameter
    Mehod body
```

Example

```
class mobile:
   @staticmethod    #decorator
    def show_model():    #static method
        print('Raelme X')
realme=mobile()
mobile.show_model()  #calling static method without argument
```

Calling static method with argument

Syntax: classname.method_name(actual parameter)

Example

```
class mobile:
   @classmethod
    def show_model(m, p):
        model=m
        price=p
        print(model, price)
realme=mobile()
mobile.show_model('RealMe X',101)  #calling static method with argument
```

Example Class variable or static variable and static method

```
class computer:
   name="dell" #class variable or static variable
   def __init__(self,ram,hd,pro):
      self.ram=ram
      self.hd=hd
      self.pro="i5"
   def feature(self):  #self as pointer it is take object atumatically
      print("your computer config is:",self.ram,self.hd,self.pro)
   @classmethod
```

```
    def company(cls):
        print("company name is:",cls.name)
    @staticmethod  #static method
    def price():
        print("the price is 45k")
com1=computer("8gb","1tb",pro="i6")    #object it means taken raw
material for making computer
com2=computer("16gb", "2tb",pro="i5")
com1.pro="i6"
computer.feature(com1) #1st method for parameter pass this is given for final
shape for computer
com2.feature()  #2nd method for parameter pass
com2.company()  #call classmethod
com2.price()  #call static method
```

Note: static method use no variable is call static method, class method use class variable and instance method use instance variable.

16.4.6 Passing Member of one Class to Another Class

```
Class student:
  #constructor
  def __init__(self, n, r):
      self.name=n
       self.roll=r
   #instance method
   def disp(self):
       print("student Name:", self.name)
       print("student Roll:", self.roll)
#user define class
class user:
   @staticmethod
   def show(s):
     print("user Name:", self.name)
     print("user Roll:", self.roll)
     s.disp()
#creating object of student class
stu=student('Rahul', 101)
user.show(stu)
```

16.4.7 Inner Class

It means class generated within the class

Example

```
class a:
    def laptop(self):
        print("i5,1tb")
    class comname:
        def name(self):
            print("dell")
lap1=a() #constator it means class name and ()
lap1.laptop() #call function
lap2=a.comname() #call inner class
lap2.name()
```

Single inheritance

Example

```
class a:
    def feature1(self):
        print("fature of 1")
    def feature2(self):
        print("feature2 of a")
class b(a):
    def feature3(self):
        print("feature1 of b")
    def feature4(self):
        print("fature2 of b")
ob1=b()
ob1.feature1()
```

Note: inheritance means kisi dusere class ki value ko kisi dusere class se access kerna it is called inheritance

Multiple inheritance

If a class is derived from more than one parent class, then it is called multiple inheritance.

```
class Father:
    def feature1(self):
        print("fature of 1")
    def feature2(self):
```

```
        print("feature2 of a")
class Mother:
    def feature3(self):
        print("feature1 of b")
    def feature4(self):
        print("fature2 of b")
class Son(Father,Mother):
    def feature5(self):
        print("feature1 of c")
    def feature6(self):
        print("fature2 of c")
ob1=Son()
ob1.feature4()
```

16.5 Multiple Level Inheritance

In multi-level inheritance, the class inherits the feature of another derived class (child class)

Example

```
class a:
    def feature1(self):
        print("fature of 1")
    def feature2(self):
        print("feature2 of a")
class b(a):
    def feature3(self):
        print("feature1 of b")
    def feature4(self):
        print("fature2 of b")
class c(b):
    def feature5(self):
        print("feature1 of c")
    def feature6(self):
        print("fature2 of c")
ob1=c()
ob1.feature1()
```

16.6 Constructor in Inheritance

By default, The constructor in the parent class is available to the child class

Example with init method

```
class a:
   def __init__(self): #constructor method
      print("hii")
   def feature1(self):
      print("fature of 1")
   def feature2(self):
      print("feature2 of a")
class b(a):
   def feature3(self):
      print("feature1 of b")
   def feature4(self):
      print("fature2 of b")
ob1=b()
ob1.feature1()
```

16.6.1 Constructor Overriding

If we write constructor in the both classes, parent class and child class then the parent class constructor is not available to child class.

In this case only child class constructor is accessible which means child class constructor is replacing parent class constructor. This concept is called overriding constructor.

Example

```
Class Father:
   def __init__(self):
      self.money=2000
      print("Father class constructor")
class Son(Father):
   def __init__(self):
      self.money=5000
      print("son class constructor")
   def disp(self):
      print(self.money)
s=Son()
s.disp()
```

16.6.2 Constructor with Super() Method

- If we write constructor in the both classes, parent class and child class then the parent class constructor is not available to the child class.
- In this case only child class constructor is accessible which means child class constructor is replacing parent class constructor. This concept is called overriding constructor.
- **super()** method is used to call parent class constructor or methods from the child class.

Example supper use command

```
class a:
   def __init__(self): #constructor method
      print("hii")
   def feature1(self):
      print("fature1 of a")
   def feature2(self):
      print("feature2 of a")
class b(a):
   def __init__(self): #constructor method
      print("bye")
      super().__init__() #this command use for calling init fuction ineritance
   def feature3(self):
      print("feature1 of b")
      super().feature1()
   def feature4(self):
      print("fature2 of b")
ob1=b()
ob1.feature3()
```

16.6.3 Method Resolution Order

In the multiple inheritance scenario members of class are searched first in the current class. If not found, the search continue into parent classed in depth first, left to right manner without searching the same class twice.

- Search for the child class before going to its parent class.
- When a class is inherited from several classes, it searches in the order from left to right in the parent classes.
- It will not visit any class more than once which means a class in the inheritance hierarchy is traversed only once exactly

Example

```
class a:
    def __init__(self): #constructor method
        print("hii")
    def feature1(self):
        print("fature1 of a")
    def feature2(self):
        print("feature2 of a")
class c:
    def __init__(self): #constructor method
        print("cc")
    def feature1(self):
        print("fature1 of c")
    def feature2(self):
        print("feature2 of c")
class b(a,c):
    def __init__(self): #constructor method

        print("bye")
        super().__init__()
    def feature3(self):
        print("feature1 of b")
    def feature4(self):
        print("fature2 of b")
ob1=b()
```

output:

```
hii
bye
```

16.7 Hierarchical Inheritance

When more than one derived classes are created from a single base this type of inheritance is called hierarchical inheritance. In this program, we have a parent (base) class and two child (derived) classes.

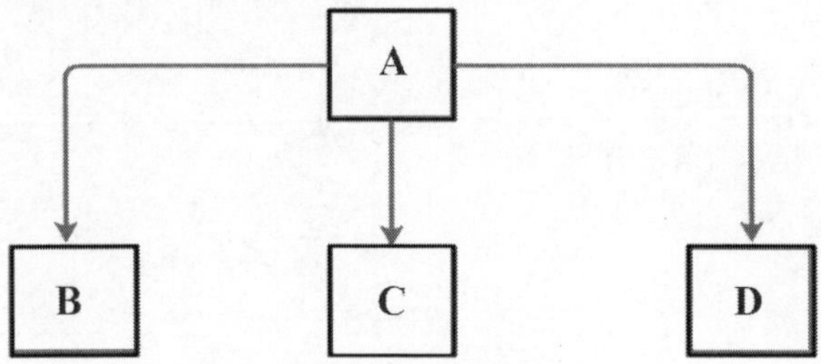

Hierarchical Inheritance

Syntax

```
Class parentclassName(object):
    Members of parent class
Class ChildclassName1(ParentClassName):
    Members of child class2
Class ChildclassName2(ParentClassName):
    Members of child class2
```

Example

```
class Father:
    def showF(self):
        print("Father class method")
class Son(Father):
    def showS(self):
        print("Son class method")
class Daughter(Father):
    def showD(self):
        print("Daughter class method")
s=Son()
s.showS()
s.showF()  #error
```

16.8 Polymorphism

If a variable, object or method perform different behaviour according to situation, it is called polymorphism.

- Duck Typing
- Operator overloading

- Method overloading
- Method overriding

16.8.1 Duck Typing

In python, we follow a principle- If 'it walks like a duck and talks like a duck, it must be a duck' which means python doesn't care about which class of object it is, if it is an object and required behaviour is present for that object then it will work. The type type of object is distinguished only at runtime. This is called as duck typing.

Python doesn't care about which class of object it is, in order to call an existing method on an object. If the method is defined on the object, then it will be called.

Walk-thapak thapak

Walk-tabdak tabdak

Example

```
class duck:
    def walk(self):
        print("thapak thapak")
clas horse:
    def walk(self):
        print("tabdak tabdak")
def myfunction(obj):
    obj.walk()
d=duck()
myfunction(d)
```

16.8.2 Strong Typing

We can check whether the object passed to the method has the method being invoked or not.

hasattr() function is used to check whether the object has a method or not.

Syntax: hasattr(object, attribute)

Where attribute can be a method or variable. If it is found in the object then this method returns True else False.

Example

```
class duck:
    def walk(self):
        print("thapak thapak")
clas horse:
    def walk(self):
        print("tabdak tabdak")
class Cat:
    def talk(self):
        print("Meow Meow")
def myfunction(obj):
    if hasattr(obj, 'walk'):
        obj.walk()
d=duck()
myfunction(d)
c=Cat()
myfunction(C)
```

16.8.3 Overriding Method in OOP

If we write method in the both classes, parent class and child class then the parent class's method is not available to the child class.

If this case only child class,s method is accessible which means child class's method is replacing parent class,s method.

Method overriding is used when programmer want to modify the existing behaviour of a method.

Overriding the methods allows a user to override the parent class method.

The name of the method must be the same in the parent class and the child class

Example

```
class first():
    def m(self): #method name same
        print("m method first class")
class second(first):
    def m(self): #method name same this concept is called overriding
        print("m method second class")
ob1=second()
ob1.m()
ob1=first()
ob1.m()
```

Note: object call different-2 class at a same time is called polymorphism

16.8.4 Overloading in Python Programming

When more than one method with the same name is defined in the same class, it is known as method overloading.

In python, if a method is written such that it can perform more than one task, it is called method overloading.

Example

```
class myclass:
    def sum(selfself,a):
        print("1st sum method",a)
    def sum(self):
        print("2nd sum method")
obj=myclass()
```

```
obj.sum()
obj.sum(10)
```

output:

2nd sum method

Note: In python overloading is not perform. If above program is run the 2nd output come and 1st output error show because last function priority is high.

17

Modules in Python Programming

17.1 Modules

- A module is a file containing python definitions and statements.
- A python module is (.py file) containing variables, class definitions, statement and function related to a particular task. The major feature of having module is that its content can be reused in other programs, without having to rewrite or recreate them.
- They are executed only the first time the module name is encounter in an import statement.

Type of modules:

- User defined modules
- Built-in modules

Ex.-array, math, numpy, sys, etc.

17.1.1 When and why use Module

- Assume that you are building a very large project, it will be very difficult to manage all logic within one single file so if you want to separate your similar logic to a separate file, you can use module.
- It will not ony separate your logics but also help you to debug your code easily as you know which logic is defined in which module.
- When a module is developed, it can be reused in any program that needs that module

17.1.2 Structure of Python Module

a. Docstring: trple quoted string for documentation purpose

b. Variable and constants

c. Classes: template/blueprint to create object

d. Object: instance of class

e. Statement: instruction

f. Function: to perform task

Note:function use within the program but module use any program using import statement.

17.1.3 Create a Module

Example

```
#addition.py
def add(a,b):
  c=a+b
  print(c)
```

How to use

```
import addition

addition.add(12,13)
```

Importing module

The import statement can be used in tow forms

a. import<module_name>

b. from<module_name>import<function_name>

c. import module_name as alias_name

d. from module_name import*

If we want show all list of function in a modules then we use dir() function. This show all function and its variables.

Note: Modules can import other other modules

17.1.4 How to Access Methods, Functions, Variable and Classes

Using the module name you can access the functions.

Syntax: module_name.function_name()

Example

```
addition.add(12,13)
```

17.2 Package in Python Programming

A package can have one or more modules which means, a package is collection of modules and packages.

A package can contain packages

Package is nothing but a directory/folder

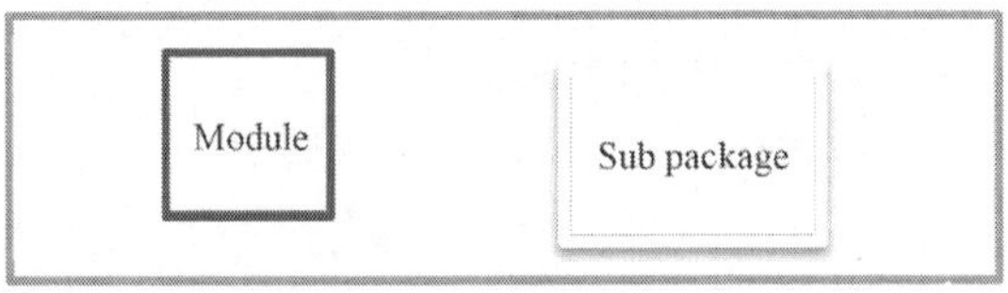

17.2.1 Creating package

Package is nothing but a directory/folder which MUST contain a special file called __init__.py

__init__.py file can be empty, it indicates that the directory it contains is a python package, so it can be imported the same way a module can be imported.

How to import package

import packageName.moduleName

Example

Import modules from single package
Pack1 folder
```
def display():
   print("this is display function in module1 ")
```
pack1 folder
```
def show():
   print("this is show function in module2 ")
```

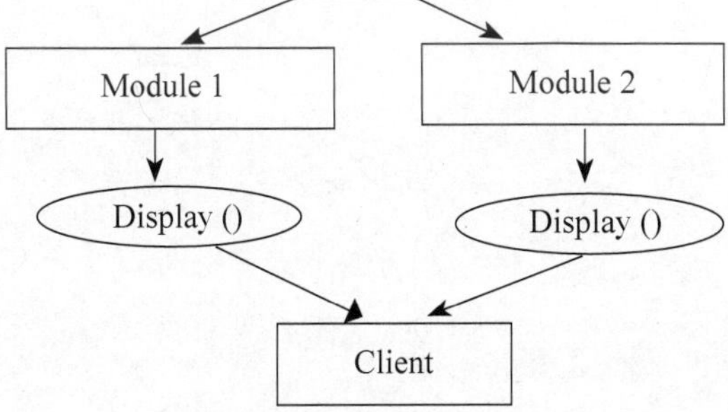

Pack2 folder

```
import sys
sys.path.append("C:/Users/AGYA VERMA/PycharmProjects/myProject/pack1")
#aproach1
import module1
import module2
module1.display()
module2.show()
#aproach2
from module1 import*
from module2 import*
display()
show()
```

Example

Import modules from two different packages

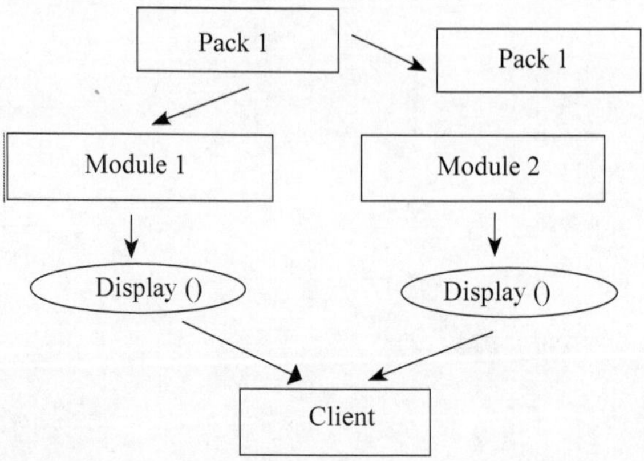


```
import sys
sys.path.append("C:/Users/AGYA VERMA/PycharmProjects/myProject/demo1")
from module1 import*
sys.path.append("C:/Users/AGYA VERMA/PycharmProjects/myProject/demo1/demo2")
from module2 import*
module1.display()
module2.show()
```

How to access variable, function, method, class etc.

packageName.moduleName.functionName()

packageName.subpackage Name.moduleName.functionName()

or

from packageName.moduleName import functionName()

from packageName.subpackage Name.moduleName import functionName()

17.3 Abstract class

- A class derived from ***ABC*** class which belongs to ***abc*** module, is known as abstract class in python.
- ABC class is known as meta class which means a class that defines the behaviour of other classes. So we can say, meta class ABC defines that the class which is derived from it becomes an abstract class.
- Abstract class can have abstract method and concrete methods.
- Abstract class needs to be extended and its and its method implemented.
- PVM can not create objects of an abstract class

Example

```
From abc import ABC, abstractmethod
        Class Father(ABC):
```

17.3.1 Abstract method

A abstract method is a method whose action is redefined in the child classes as per the requirement of the object.

We can declare a method as abstract by using @abstractmethod decorator

Example

```
From abc import ABC, abstractmethod
Class Father(ABC): #abstract class
   @abstractmethod
    def disp(self):  #abstract method
        pass
```

17.3.2 Concrete Method

A concrete method is a method whose action is defined in the abstract class itself.

Example

```
From abc import ABC, abstractmethod
Class Father(ABC):  #abstract class
    @abstractmethod
    def disp(self):   #abstract method
        pass
    def show(self):   #concrete method
      print("concrete Method")
class child(Father):
      def disp(self):
          print("child class")
          print("defing abstract method")
c=child()
c.disp()
c.show()
```

Rules

- PVM can not create objects of an abstract class.
- It is not necessary to declare all methods abstract in a abstract class
- Abstract class can have abstract method and concrete methods
- If there is any abstract method in a class, that class must be abstract.
- The abstract methods of an abstract class must be defined in its child class/subclass.
- If you are inheriting abstract class that have abstract method, you must either provide the implementation of the method or make this class abstract.

When use abstract class

We use abstract class when there are some common feature shared by all the objects as they are

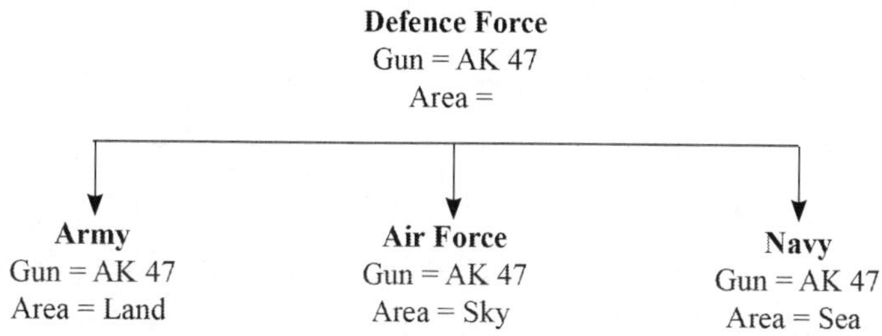

17.4 Interface

In python, the interface concept is not explicity available, like available in other language e.g. Java

In python, an interface is an abstract class which contains only abstract method but not a single concrete method

Example

```
From abc import ABC, abstractmethod
Class Father(ABC):  #abstract class
    @abstractmethod
     def disp(self):   #abstract method
         pass
class child(Father):
       def disp(self):
           print("child class")
           print("defing abstract method")
c=child()
c.disp()
```

Rules

- All methods of an interface is abstract.
- We can not create object of interface.
- If a class is implementing an interface it has to define all the methods given in that interface.
- If a class does not implement all the methods declared in the interface, the class must be declared abstract.

When use interface

We use interface when all the feature need to be implemented differently for different object.

17.5 Data Hiding in Python

We use double underscore (__) before the attributes name and those attributes are hide from other classes in the program.

a=10 (public in the program
_a=10 (protected)
__a=10 (private)

Example

```
class arv:
    __secretverma=0 #data member is hiding by prefixing two__ it means
private variable
  def verma(self):
      self.__secretverma+=1
      print(self.__secretverma)
obj=arv()
obj.verma()
obj.verma()
print(obj._arv__secretverma) # you can access hide data member by object
with using class
#print(obj.__secretverma) # without using class name, object can not access
hide data member and show
```

17.6 Error in Python

Errors are the problems in a program due to which the program will stop the execution. On the other hand, exceptions are raised when some internal events occur which changes the normal flow of the program.

Two types of Error occurs in python.

- Syntax errors
- Logical errors (Exceptions)

17.7 Exception in Python

An exception is a runtime error which can be handled by the programmer.

All exception are represented as classes in python

17.7.1 Type of Exception

(i) Built in exception: Exception which are already available in python language. The base class for all built-in exception is base exception class.

(ii) User defined exception: A programmer can create his own exception, called user-defined exceptions.

17.7.2 Need of Exception Handling

- When an exception occurs, the program terminates suddenly.
- Suddenly termination of program may corrupt the program.
- Exception may cause data loss from the database or a file

17.7.3 Exception Handling

Try – the try block contains code which may cause exceptions.

Syntax:

```
try:
   statement
```

Except- The except block is used to catch an exception that is raised in the try block. There can be multiple except block for try block.

Syntax:

```
Except Exception Name
```

Else-this block will get executed when no exception is raised. Else block is executed after try block.

Syntax:

```
Else:
  Statement
```

Finally-this block will get execute irrespective of whether there is an exception or not

Syntax:

```
Finally:
  statement
```

Some points for exception handling

- We can write several except block for a single try block.
- We can write multiple except blocks to handle multiple exceptions.
- We can write try block without any except blocks.
- We cannot write except block without a try block.
- Finally block is always executed irrespective of whether there is an exception or not.
- Else block is optional.
- Finally block is optional

Example

```
a=10
b=5
d=a/0
print(d)
print('rest of the code')
```

output:

exception error

zerodivisionerror:division by zero

Note: program terminate

Handling exception

Example

```
a=10
b=0
try:
   d=a/b
   print(d)
except:
   print("division by zero not allowed")
print('rest of code')
```

output:

division by zero not allowed

rest of code

Note: it means program is not terminate

Example

```
a=10
b=0
try:
   d=a/b
   print(d)
except:
   print("division by zero not allowed")
else:
   print('inside else') #if exception occur then this line not run
finally:
   print('inside finally') # this line always run
print('rest of code')
```

output:

division by zero not allowed

inside finally

rest of code

17.7.4 User Defined Exception

A programmer can create his own exception, called user-defined exceptions.

- creating exception class using exception class as a base class
- raising exception
- handling exception

17.7.5 Creating Exception

we can create our own exception by creating a sub class to built-in exception class:

syntax:

```
class MyException(exception):
   pass
class MyException(Exception):
   def __init__(self, arg):
```

17.7.6 Raising Exception

Raise statement is used to raise the user defined exception

Syntax:

Raise MyException(exception)

Handling Exception: using try and except block programmer can handle exception

Syntax:

```
try:
  statement
except MyException as mye:
statement
```

Example User define exception make, raise and handling

```
class BalanceException(Exception):
   pass
def checkbalance():
   money=10000
   withdraw=9000
   try:
      balance=money - withdraw
      if(balance<=2000):
         raise BalanceException('Insuficent balance') # raise exception
      print(balance)
   except BalanceException as be:
      print(be)
checkbalance()
```

output:

Insuficent balance

18

Python Library

18.1 Library Introduction

This library contains modules for various types of functionalities. Some commonly use module of python standard library are:

(i) math module: which provides mathematical function to support difference types of calaculations.

(ii) cmath modules: which provides mathematical function for complex number.

(iii) random module: which provides function generation random number.

(iv) staticstics module: which provides mathematical satical function.

(v) urllib module: which provides URL handling function so that you can access websites from within your program.

1. NmPy library, provides some advance math functionalities along with tools to create and manipulate numeric arrays.
2. Scipy library, provides algorithmic and mathematical tools for scientific calculations.
3. Tkinter library, provides python user interface toolkit and helps you to create user friendly GUI for different types of applications.
4. Matplotlib library, provides functins and tools to produce quality output in variety of formats such as plots, charts, graphs, ete.

18.1.1 Brief Tour of the Standard Library

GUI programming in python

You would have used a lot of applications. One common thing you observe in all the applications is that they have multiple components like labels, fields to give inputs, buttons, etc. These are the elements that form the GUI (Graphical User Interface).

In this chapter, we will learn to make GUIs using Python. We will see different toolkits that Python provides for GUI programming. Then we will discuss the Tkinter, one of the most commonly used modules, in detail.

Let us start by seeing different modules Python offers.

Python Libraries for GUI Programming

We can use any of the following toolkits in Python for GUI programming.

1. Tkinter: Tkinter is a standard package used for GUI programming in Python. This is built on top of the Tk interface.
2. PyQt:PyQt is a Python toolkit binding of the Qt toolkit. Qt is a C++ framework that is used by Python to implement a cross-platform PyQt toolkit as a plug-in.
3. wxPython: wxPython is also a cross-platform GUI toolkit. It is a wrapper for the API wxWidgets.

18.1.2 Python Tkinter Module

Tkinter tutorial provides basic and advanced concepts of Python Tkinter. In this chapter is designed for beginners and professionals.

Python provides the standard library Tkinter for creating the graphical user interface for desktop based applications.

Developing desktop based applications with python Tkinter is not a complex task. An empty Tkinter top-level window can be created by using the following steps.

1. import the Tkinter module.
2. Create the main application window.
3. Add the widgets like labels, buttons, frames, etc. to the window.
4. Call the main event loop so that the actions can take place on the user's computer screen.

Example

```
from tkinter import *
root=Tk()
root.title("My First Window")
label=Label(root, font=("Ariel",45),text="enter your
name",bg="yellow",fg="blue")
label.pack()
```

```
root.geometry("400x500+300+150")
root.resizable(0,0)
root.mainloop()
```

18.2 Tkinter Widgets

There are various widgets like button, canvas, checkbutton, entry, etc. that are used to build the python GUI applications.

S.N	Widget	Description
1	Button	The Button is used to add various kinds of buttons to the python application.
2	Canvas	The canvas widget is used to draw the canvas on the window.
3	Checkbutton	The Checkbutton is used to display the CheckButton on the window.
4	Entry	The entry widget is used to display the single-line text field to the user. It is commonly used to accept user values.
5	Frame	It can be defined as a container to which, another widget can be added and organized.
6	Label	A label is a text used to display some message or information about the other widgets.
7	ListBox	The ListBox widget is used to display a list of options to the user.
8	Menubutton	The Menubutton is used to display the menu items to the user.
9	Menu	It is used to add menu items to the user.
10	Message	The Message widget is used to display the message-box to the user.
11	Radiobutton	The Radiobutton is different from a checkbutton. Here, the user is provided with various options and the user can select only one option among them.
12	Scale	It is used to provide the slider to the user.
13	Scrollbar	It provides the scrollbar to the user so that the user can scroll the window up and down.
14	Text	It is different from Entry because it provides a multi-line text field to the user so that the user can write the text and edit the text inside it.
14	Toplevel	It is used to create a separate window container.
15	Spinbox	It is an entry widget used to select from options of values.
16	PanedWindow	It is like a container widget that contains horizontal or vertical panes.
17	LabelFrame	A LabelFrame is a container widget that acts as the container
18	MessageBox	This module is used to display the message-box in the desktop based applications.

18.3 Python Tkinter Geometry

The Tkinter geometry specifies the method by using which, the widgets are represented on display. The python Tkinter provides the following geometry methods.

1. The pack() method
2. The grid() method
3. The place() method

Let's discuss each one of them in detail.

18.3.1 Python Tkinter Pack() Method

The pack() widget is used to organize widget in the block. The positions widgets added to the python application using the pack() method can be controlled by using the various options specified in the method call.

However, the controls are less and widgets are generally added in the less organized manner.

The syntax to use the pack() is given below.

Syntax: widget.pack(options)

A list of possible options that can be passed in pack() is given below.

- **expand:** If the expand is set to true, the widget expands to fill any space.
- **Fill:** By default, the fill is set to NONE. However, we can set it to X or Y to determine whether the widget contains any extra space.
- **size:** it represents the side of the parent to which the widget is to be placed on the window.

Example

```
from tkinter import *

parent = Tk()

redbutton = Button(parent, text = “Red”, fg = “red”)

redbutton.pack( side = LEFT)

greenbutton = Button(parent, text = “Black”, fg = “black”)

greenbutton.pack( side = RIGHT )

bluebutton = Button(parent, text = “Blue”, fg = “blue”)
```

```
bluebutton.pack( side = TOP )
blackbutton = Button(parent, text = "Green", fg = "red")
blackbutton.pack( side = BOTTOM)
parent.mainloop()
```

Output

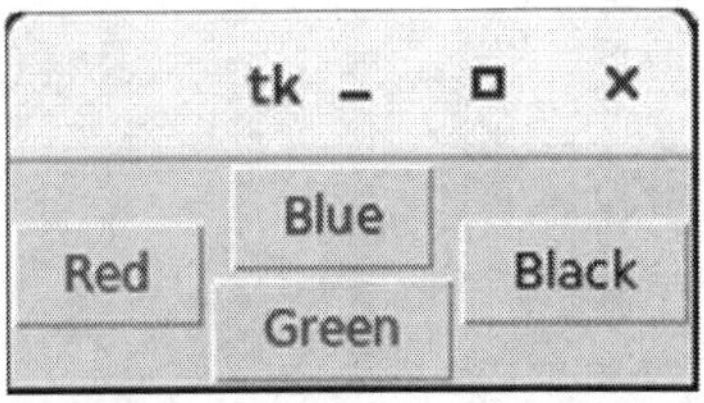

18.3.2 Python Tkinter Grid() Method

The grid() geometry manager organizes the widgets in the tabular form. We can specify the rows and columns as the options in the method call. We can also specify the column span (width) or rowspan(height) of a widget.

This is a more organized way to place the widgets to the python application. The syntax to use the grid() is given below.

Syntax: widget.grid(options)

A list of possible options that can be passed inside the grid() method is given below.

- **Column**: The column number in which the widget is to be placed. The leftmost column is represented by 0.
- **Columnspan**: The width of the widget. It represents the number of columns up to which, the column is expanded.
- **ipadx, ipady**: It represents the number of pixels to pad the widget inside the widget's border.
- **padx, pady**: It represents the number of pixels to pad the widget outside the widget's border.
- **Row**: The row number in which the widget is to be placed. The topmost row is represented by 0.

- **Rowspan**: The height of the widget, i.e. the number of the row up to which the widget is expanded.
- **Sticky**: If the cell is larger than a widget, then sticky is used to specify the position of the widget inside the cell. It may be the concatenation of the sticky letters representing the position of the widget. It may be N, E, W, S, NE, NW, NS, EW, ES.

Example

```
# !/usr/bin/python3
from tkinter import *
parent = Tk()
name = Label(parent,text = "Name").grid(row = 0, column = 0)
e1 = Entry(parent).grid(row = 0, column = 1)
password = Label(parent,text = "Password").grid(row = 1, column = 0)
e2 = Entry(parent).grid(row = 1, column = 1)
submit = Button(parent, text = "Submit").grid(row = 4, column = 0)
parent.mainloop()
```

Output

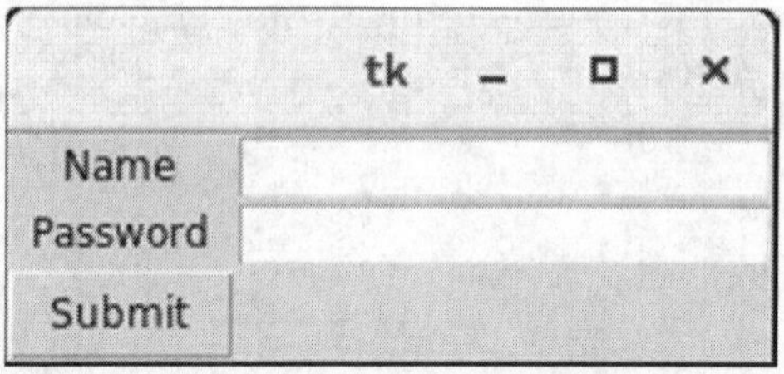

18.3.3 Python Tkinter Place() Method

The place() geometry manager organizes the widgets to the specific x and y coordinates.

Syntax:widget.place(options)

A list of possible options is given below.

- **Anchor:** It represents the exact position of the widget within the container. The default value (direction) is NW (the upper left corner).
- **bordermode:** The default value of the border type is INSIDE that refers to ignore the parent›s inside the border. The other option is OUTSIDE.
- **height, width:** It refers to the height and width in pixels.

- **relheight, relwidth:** It is represented as the float between 0.0 and 1.0 indicating the fraction of the parent›s height and width.
- **relx, rely:** It is represented as the float between 0.0 and 1.0 that is the offset in the horizontal and vertical direction.
- **x, y:** It refers to the horizontal and vertical offset in the pixels.

Example

```
# !/usr/bin/python3
from tkinter import *
top = Tk()
top.geometry("400x250")
name = Label(top, text = "Name").place(x = 30,y = 50)
email = Label(top, text = "Email").place(x = 30, y = 90)
password = Label(top, text = "Password").place(x = 30, y = 130)
e1 = Entry(top).place(x = 80, y = 50)
e2 = Entry(top).place(x = 80, y = 90)
e3 = Entry(top).place(x = 95, y = 130)
top.mainloop()
```

Output

19

Turtle Graphics

19.1 Python Turtle Graphics

Turtle is a special feathers of Python. Using Turtle, we can easily draw in a drawing board.

First we import the turtle module. Then create a window, next we create turtle object and using turtle method we can draw in the drawing board.

19.2 Some Turtle Method

Method	Parameter	Description
Turtle()	None	It creates and returns a new turtle object
forward()	amount	It moves the turtle forward by the specified amount
backward()	amount	It moves the turtle backward by the specified amount
right()	angle	It turns the turtle clockwise
left()	angle	It turns the turtle counter clockwise
penup()	None	It picks up the turtle's Pen
pendown()	None	Puts down the turtle's Pen
up()	None	Picks up the turtle's Pen
down()	None	Puts down the turtle's Pen
color()	Color name	Changes the color of the turtle's pen
fillcolor()	Color name	Changes the color of the turtle will use to fill a polygon
heading()	None	It returns the current heading
position()	None	It returns the current position
goto()	x, y	It moves the turtle to position x,y
begin_fill()	None	Remember the starting point for a filled polygon
end_fill()	None	It closes the polygon and fills with the current fill color
dot()	None	Leaves the dot at the current position
stamp()	None	Leaves an impression of a turtle shape at the current location
shape()	shapename	Should be 'arrow', 'classic', 'turtle' or 'circle'

Example

```
from turtle import *
t = Turtle()   #object in python
wn=Screen()
```

```
wn.title("my first graphic")
wn.bgcolor("yellow")  #color filling in window
t.shape("turtle")     #turtle shape given
t.color("red", "green")
t.speed(1)        #turtle speed given
t.begin_fill()
for i in range(4):
   t.forward(100)
   t.left(90)
t.penup()    #pen up
t.forward(200)
t.pendown()
for i in range(4):
   t.forward(100)
   t.left(90)
t.end_fill()
done()
```

20

Brief Tour of the Standard Library

20.1 Unit Testing in Python Programming

The process of testing wheather a particular unit is working properly or not is called unit testing. A unit test checks small component in your application

Example

```
def testsum1():
    assert sum([1,2,3])==6
def testsum2():
assert sum([1,1,1])==6   #assertion error
testsum1()
testsum2()
```

20.1.1 Step Involved in Unit Testing

(1) Import unittest from library.

(2) Create a class for test and inherit (unittest.TestCase).

(3) Write the test function in the class.

(4) Call unittest.main()

20.1.2 Writing Test Cases & Running Tests

Example

```
import unittest
class Testsum(unittest.TestCase):
  def testsum1(self):
    self.assertEqual(sum([1,2,3]),6)
  def testsum2(self):
    self.assertEqual(sum([1,2,2]),6)
unittest.main()
```

output

AssertionError: 5 != 6

Example 2

```
import unittest
class Testsum(unittest.TestCase):
   def testsum1(self):
      self.assertEqual(sum([1,2,3]),6)
   def testsum2(self):
      self.assertEqual(sum([1,2,2]),5)
unittest.main()
```

output:

No error

20.2 Thread in Python Programming

Thread is a separate flow of execution. Every thread has a task

20.2.1 Multithreading

Using multiple threads in program or process

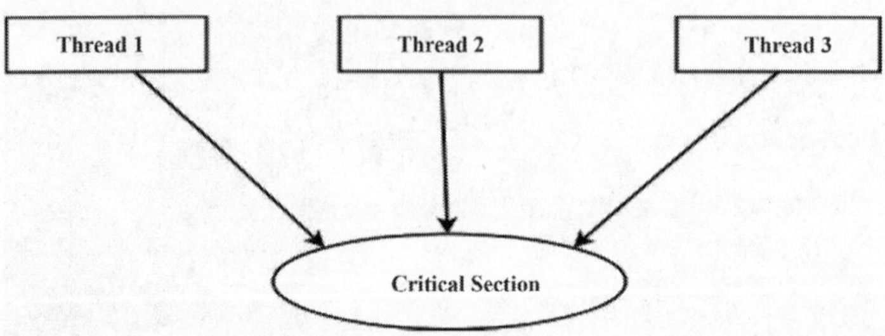

The main important application areas of multi threading are:

- Multimedia graphic
- Animations
- Video games
- Web servers
- Application servers

20.3 Error vs Exception

- An exception is an error that can be handled by a programmer.

- An exception which are not handled by programmer, becomes an error.
- All exception occur only at runtime.
- Error may occur at compile time or runtime.

Data compression:

with help of zlib.compress(s) and bzz.compress(s) we can get compress the bytes of string

Syntax: zlib.compress(string), bzz.compress(string)

Example

```
import zlib
s=”welcome to python”
print(s)
print(len(s)) #output 18
t=zlib.compress(s)
print(t)
print(len(t))     #output 26
import bzz
t=bzz.compress(s)
print(t)
print(len(t)) #output 53
```

20.4 Operating System Interface in Python

The OS module provides many variables and functions for interacting with the operating system.

- os.name is either ‘posix’ or ‘nt’
- os.curdir is a string representing the current directory (always ‘.’)
- os.pardir is a string representing the parent directory (always ‘..’)
- os.sep is the (or a most common) pathname separator (‘/’ or ‘\\’)
- os.extsep is the extension separator (always ‘.’)
- os.pathsep is the component separator used in $PATH etc
- os.defpath is the default search path for executables
- os.cpu_count()

Return the number of CPUs in the system; return None if indeterminable.

- os.listdir()

  Return a list containing the names of the files in the directory.

- os.getcwd()

  Return a unicode string representing the current working directory.

- os.getcwdb()

  Return a bytes string representing the current working directory.

- os.chdir()

  Change the current working directory to the specified path.

- os.system('mkdir today')
- os.system(command)

  Execute the command in a subshell.

- os.renames(old, new): change the name of the file

Example

```
import platform
>>> platform.system()
'Windows'
>>> platform.release()
'8'
```

Example

```
#create floder in c drive with name itutees
import os,platform
print(os.name)
print(platform.system())
print(platform.release())
print(os.curdir)#'.'
print(os.pardir)#'..'
print(os.sep)#'\'
print(os.extsep)#'.'
print(os.pathsep)#';'
print(os.defpath)#'.;C:\bin'
print(os.cpu_count())
```

```
print(os.listdir())
print(os.getcwd())
print(os.getcwdb())
print(os.chdir('C:\itutees'))
print(os.getcwd())
os.system('mkdir xyz')
os.renames('xyz','abc')
```

20.4.1 String Pattern Matching

The re module provides regular expression tools for advanced string processing

Function –import re

findall(): #returns a list containing all matches

Example

```
s="itutees channel"
f=re.findall("[a-f]",s) #A set of characters
print(f)
search(): #returns a list where the string has been split at each match
```

Example

```
s="welcome to 123"
f=re.search("\d",s)
print(f.start())
split(): #returns a list where the string match with a string
s="welcome to itutees"
f=re.split("\s",s)
print(f)
sub(): #Replaces one or many matches with a string
s="welcome to itutees"
f=re.sub("\s","*",s)
print(f)
metacharacters
characters with a special meaning
[] a set characters
s="itutees channel"
f=re.findall("[a-f]",s) #A set of characters
print(f)
\ signals a special sequence
```

```
s="itutees 123"
f=re.findall("\d",s)
print(f)
. any character(except newline character)
s="welcome to itutees"
f=re.findall("it....s",s)
print(f)
^ starts with
s="welcome to itutees"
f=re.findall("^welcome",s)
print(f)
$ ends with
s="welcome to itutees"
f=re.findall("itutees$",s)
print(f)
            * Zero or more occurences
s="The ran in spain"
f=re.findall("ai*",s)
print(f)
            + Zero or more occurences
s="welcome to itutees"
f=re.findall("ai+",s)
print(f)
        {}  exactly the specify number of occurance
s="welcome to itutees"
f=re.findall("te{2}",s)
print(f)
   : either or
s='good boy'
f=re.findall("good|nice",s)
print(f)
```

20.5 Datetime Module

- datetime- it handles date and time. It has year, month, day, hour, minute, second, microsecond and tzinfo attributes
- date-it handle dates of Gregorian clender, without taking time zone into consideration. It has year month and day attributes.
- Time-it handles time assuming that every day has exactly 24x60x60 seconds. It has hour, minute, second, microsecond and tzinfo attributes.

- Timedelta-it handles durations. The duration may be the difference between two date time or datetime instances.
- datetime object-a datetime object is a single object containing all the information from a date object and a time object.

20.5.1 Creating Object of Datetime Class

Object_name=datetime(year, month, day, hour=0, minute=0, second=0, microsencd=0, tzinfo=None, *, fold=0)

The year, month and day arguments are required. Tzinfo may be none, or an instance of a tzinfo subclass. The remaining arguments may be integers, in the following ranges:

fold in [0, 1]

the fold parameter specifies whether there was any fold in time. A fold in time means a reverse back of the clock time. In countries following Daylight saving time during the end of summer clocks are reversed back by 1 hour. This reverse back is a fold in time

* mean a splat operator. Using s splat plot operator a tuple can be unpacks and a time object can be constructed out of the value from the tuple.

Exmple

```
from datetime import datetime
dt=datetime(year=2019, month=6, day=30)
dt1=datetime(2016, 6, 25, 14, 30)
print(dt)
print(dt1)
```

now() – this method is used to get the current date and time. We can provide timezone information to this method. If the timezone is not provided, then ot takes the local time zone. It returns an object that contains date information in any timezone. We can use day, month, year, hour, minute and second

Example

Syntax: datetime.now()
today()-this method is used to get the current date and time. It returns the date and time information.
Ex: datetime.today()

Example

```
from datetime import datetime
ct=datetime.now()
print(ct)
print(ct.year)
output:
2021-12-05 14:18:49.826925
2021
```

20.5.2 Date Class

Date object- A date object is an object containging information of year, month and day

Creating object of date class

Syntax:

Object_name=date(year, month, day)

All argument are required. Arguments may be integers and fallowing ranges:

Example

D=date(year=2019, month=6, day=30)
Date class's method

Example

```
from datetime import date
ct=date(year=2021, month=12, day=5)
cd=date.day()
print(ct)
print(cd)
```

20.5.3 Time Class

time object – a time object is an object containing information of local time of day, independent of any particular day and subject to adjustment via a tzinfo object

syntax:

Creating object of time class

Object_name=time(hour=0, minute=0, second=0, microsencd=0, tzinfo=None, *, fold=0)

All argument are optional. tzinfo may be none or an instance of a tzinfo subclass. The remaining argument may be integers

Example

```
from datetime import time
ct=time(hour=20, minute=12, second=5)
print(ct)
print(ct.hour)
```

20.5.4 Timedelta Class in Python

- timedelta object-a timedelta object represent a duration, the difference between two dates or times.
- it is possible to know the future dates or previous dates using timedelta

syntax:

Creating object of time class

Object_name=timedelta(days=0, seconds=0, miroseconds=0, miniseconds=0, minutes=0, hours=0, weeks=0)

All argument are optional and default to 0. Argument may be integers or floats and may be positive or negative

Only days, seconds and microseconds are stored internally. Argument are converted to those units:

A miliseconds is converted to 1000 microseconds

A minute is converted to 60 seconds

A hour is converted to 3600 seconds

A week is converted to 7 days

Example

```
from datetime import timedelta, date

ct=timedelta(days=10)

d=date.today()

print(ct)

print(d)

print(d+ct)
```

20.6 Math Module in Python

- It is a module that contains several function to perform mathematical operation.
- If we want to use this module then we have to import it first from mat import *

20.7 Numbers and Numeric Representation

Sr.No.	Function & Description
1	ceil(x) Return the Ceiling value. It is the smallest integer, greater or equal to the number x.
2	copysign(x, y) It returns the number x and copy the sign of y to x.
3	fabs(x) Returns the absolute value of x.
4	factorial(x) Returns factorial of x. where $x \geq 0$
5	floor(x) Return the Floor value. It is the largest integer, less or equal to the number x.
6	fsum(iterable) Find sum of the elements in an iterable object
7	gcd(x, y) Returns the Greatest Common Divisor of x and y
8	isfinite(x) Checks whether x is neither an infinity nor nan.
9	isinf(x) Checks whether x is infinity
10	isnan(x) Checks whether x is not a number.
11	remainder(x, y) Find remainder after dividing x by y.

These functions are used to represent numbers in different forms. The methods are like below

Example

```
import math
print('The Floor and Ceiling value of 23.56 are: ' + str(math.ceil(23.56)) + ',
' + str(math.floor(23.56)))
x = 10
y = -15
print('The value of x after copying the sign from y is: ' + str(math.
copysign(x, y)))
```

```
print('Absolute value of -96 and 56 are: ' + str(math.fabs(-96)) + ', ' +
str(math.fabs(56)))
my_list = [12, 4.25, 89, 3.02, -65.23, -7.2, 6.3]
print('Sum of the elements of the list: ' + str(math.fsum(my_list)))
print('The GCD of 24 and 56 : ' + str(math.gcd(24, 56)))
x = float('nan')
if math.isnan(x):
   print('It is not a number')
x = float('inf')
y = 45
if math.isinf(x):
   print('It is Infinity')
print(math.isfinite(x)) #x is not a finite number
print(math.isfinite(y)) #y is a finite number
```

output:

```
The Floor and Ceiling value of 23.56 are: 24, 23

The value of x after copying the sign from y is: -10.0

Absolute value of -96 and 56 are: 96.0, 56.0

Sum of the elements of the list: 42.13999999999999

The GCD of 24 and 56 : 8

It is not a number

It is Infinity

False

True
```

20.8 Power and Logarithmic Functions

These functions are used to calculate different power related and logarithmic related tasks.

Sr.No.	Function & Description
1	pow(x, y) Return the x to the power y value.
2	sqrt(x) Finds the square root of x
3	exp(x) Finds xe, where e = 2.718281

4	log(x[, base]) Returns the Log of x, where base is given. The default base is e
5	log2(x) Returns the Log of x, where base is 2
6	log10(x) Returns the Log of x, where base is 10

Example

```
import math
print('The value of 5^8: ' + str(math.pow(5, 8)))
print('Square root of 400: ' + str(math.sqrt(400)))
print('The value of 5^e: ' + str(math.exp(5)))
print('The value of Log(625), base 5: ' + str(math.log(625, 5)))
print('The value of Log(1024), base 2: ' + str(math.log2(1024)))
print('The value of Log(1024), base 10: ' + str(math.log10(1024)))
```

output:

```
The value of 5^8: 390625.0
Square root of 400: 20.0
The value of 5^e: 148.4131591025766
The value of Log(625), base 5: 4.0
The value of Log(1024), base 2: 10.0
The value of Log(1024), base 10: 3.010299956639812
```

20.9 Trigonometric & Angular Conversion Functions

These functions are used to calculate different trigonometric operations.

Sr.No.	Function & Description
1	sin(x) Return the sine of x in radians
2	cos(x) Return the cosine of x in radians
3	tan(x) Return the tangent of x in radians
4	asin(x) This is the inverse operation of the sine, there are acos, atan also.
5	degrees(x) Convert angle x from radian to degrees
6	radians(x) Convert angle x from degrees to radian

Example

```
import math
print('The value of Sin(60 degree): ' + str(math.sin(math.radians(60))))
print('The value of cos(pi): ' + str(math.cos(math.pi)))
print('The value of tan(90 degree): ' + str(math.tan(math.pi/2)))
print('The angle of sin(0.8660254037844386): ' + str(math.degrees(math.
asin(0.8660254037844386))))
```

output:

```
The value of Sin(60 degree): 0.8660254037844386
The value of cos(pi): -1.0
The value of tan(90 degree): 1.633123935319537e+16
The angle of sin(0.8660254037844386): 59.99999999999999
```